T0323985

Cambridge Elements

Elements in Ancient East Asia
SOURCES: Excavated Texts and Other New Sources of Data
edited by
Erica Fox Brindley
Pennsylvania State University
Rowan Kimon Flad
Harvard University

RECONSTRUCTING THE HUMAN POPULATION HISTORY OF EAST ASIA THROUGH ANCIENT GENOMICS

E. Andrew Bennett
Chinese Academy of Sciences
Yichen Liu
Chinese Academy of Sciences
Qiaomei Fu
Chinese Academy of Sciences

Shaftesbury Road, Cambridge CB2 8EA, United Kingdom

One Liberty Plaza, 20th Floor, New York, NY 10006, USA

477 Williamstown Road, Port Melbourne, VIC 3207, Australia

314–321, 3rd Floor, Plot 3, Splendor Forum, Jasola District Centre, New Delhi – 110025, India

103 Penang Road, #05–06/07, Visioncrest Commercial, Singapore 238467

Cambridge University Press is part of Cambridge University Press & Assessment, a department of the University of Cambridge.

We share the University's mission to contribute to society through the pursuit of education, learning and research at the highest international levels of excellence.

www.cambridge.org
Information on this title: www.cambridge.org/9781009517058

DOI: 10.1017/9781009246675

First published 2024

A catalogue record for this publication is available from the British Library

ISBN 978-1-009-51705-8 Hardback
ISBN 978-1-009-24664-4 Paperback
ISSN 2632-7325 (online)
ISSN 2632-7317 (print)

Reconstructing the Human Population History of East Asia through Ancient Genomics

Elements in Ancient East Asia

DOI: 10.1017/9781009246675
First published online: November 2024

E. Andrew Bennett
Chinese Academy of Sciences

Yichen Liu
Chinese Academy of Sciences

Qiaomei Fu
Chinese Academy of Sciences

Author for correspondence: E. Andrew Bennett, e.andrew.bennett@ivpp.ac.cn and Qiaomei Fu, fuqiaomei@ivpp.ac.cn

Abstract: East Asian population history has only recently been the focus of intense investigations using ancient genomics techniques, yet these studies have already contributed much to our growing understanding of past East Asian populations, and cultural and linguistic dispersals. This Element aims to provide a comprehensive overview of our current understanding of the population history of East Asia through ancient genomics. It begins with an introduction to ancient DNA and recent insights into archaic populations of East Asia. It then presents an in-depth summary of current knowledge by region, covering the whole of East Asia from the first appearance of modern humans, through large-scale population studies of the Neolithic and Metal Ages, and into historical times. These recent results reflect past population movements and admixtures, as well as linguistic origins and prehistoric cultural networks that have shaped the region's history. This title is also available as Open Access on Cambridge Core.

Keywords: East Asia, paleogenomics, migration, human origins, population history

ISBNs: 9781009517058 (HB), 9781009246644 (PB), 9781009246675 (OC)
ISSNs: 2632-7325 (online), 2632-7317 (print)

Contents

Introduction

One decade ago, the first genomic information from an early modern human from East Asia was retrieved. The Upper Paleolithic individual from Tianyuan 田园 cave near modern-day Beijing (Fu *et al.* 2013), established a genetic continuity between present-day populations and their earliest modern human ancestors in East Asia. Since then, researchers have begun progressively exploring past East Asian populations through ancient genomics, and have been building an increasingly detailed framework of the structure and interactions of prehistoric populations in East Asia over time. In this relatively short period, increasingly larger numbers of ancient nuclear genomes from East Asia have become available across multiple time-depths from diverse corners of nearly the entire East Asian region. The results of these analyses have already had profound impacts on our understanding not just of initial peopling and past migration events, but also of language dispersals, cultural exchange networks, and genetic adaptation, that have shaped the history of the region and beyond. Much information is still missing, however, and the small amount of available data and large geo-temporal gaps currently limit our knowledge of the Paleolithic Period. Also, a number of important cultures and regions have yet to be characterized genetically. Many of these investigations, however, have turned up intriguing hints and connections that require additional studies to clarify. An informed genetic landscape of East Asian diversity and admixture is nevertheless beginning to take shape.

Reconstructing ancient human population movements and interactions of East Asia through the study of ancient DNA has lagged behind the detailed understanding these studies have produced in other areas of Eurasia, notably in Europe and the Near East. The early focus on western Eurasia can be traced to the development of these techniques by predominantly European-based laboratories and the networks of archeologists with whom they interacted. Difficulties overcoming modern human contamination using early technologies limited some of the earliest questions of human origins to focus on the genetic relationship of modern humans to the Neanderthals (Green *et al.* 2006, 2008, 2010; Noonan *et al.* 2006; Wall & Kim 2007). Although the known Neanderthal range stretched as far east as Siberia, they have not been found in East Asia. Yet it was in the context of the genetic exploration of Neanderthals and ancient anatomically modern humans in Siberia that a novel hominin genome was discovered (Reich *et al.* 2010). This discovery, solely through ancient genomics, of a previously unknown archaic human population inhabiting Denisova Cave in Siberia, popularly referred to as Denisovans, was a dramatic proof of the limits of our understanding of the past through conventional archeology and morphological variation of skeletal material. The concurrent discoveries that Denisovan DNA contributed to the genomes of modern human populations still living in Oceania, East Asia, and the Americas (Reich *et al.* 2010), as well as the more recent finding that some of the earliest modern humans in Europe were genetically closer to East Asians than to present-day Europeans (Prüfer *et al.* 2021), signify the important role that East Asian population history will play as we attempt to piece together the migrations and admixture events our ancestors underwent along the way toward the evolution of modern human genomes.

This Element will explore the recent results based on ancient genomes that researchers around the world have brought to our understanding of past populations of East Asia, from initial peopling events to later demographic movements in response to climatic and technological changes. We will begin with a general overview of the challenges of recovering ancient DNA from the various East Asian climates. We will then summarize recent findings across East Asia, focusing on the major regions that have been studied to date with the goal of understanding the interrelations among the growing body of recent work. The uneven time periods currently considered in these studies, from the Paleolithic until historical times, favor a regional approach rather than a comprehensive synthesis of cross-regional trends for a given time-period. Wherever possible, links will be made between regions where adequate overlaps exist.

Challenges of Ancient DNA

The difficulty in recovering and analyzing authentic ancient DNA fragments from degraded organic material has been well described in the literature (*e.g.* (Briggs *et al.* 2007; Dabney *et al.* 2013; Kistler *et al.* 2017; Pruvost *et al.* 2007)). These and other studies have revealed that the preservation of DNA molecules over time is a result of postmortem putrefaction phases followed by the effects that environmental conditions such as temperature, humidity, salinity, and pH have on the frequency of random processes leading to strand breakage, oxidation damage, and cytosine deamination. In addition, the element of time allows the accumulation of these events, resulting in increasingly shorter molecules and an increasing amount of base-altering lesions (Allentoft *et al.* 2012; Deagle *et al.* 2006). The hot and humid environment in southern East Asia in particular has been described as especially unfavorable for the recovery of ancient DNA (Kistler *et al.* 2017; Wang *et al.* 2021a). The high level of exogenous environmental DNA relative to ancient endogenous DNA typically co-recovered from ancient material, which can often exceed 99%, also decreases the overall efficiency and substantially raises the expense of ancient DNA recovery. Discoveries in the last decade of the exceptional DNA preservation often encountered within the dense inner part of the petrous bone (Gamba *et al.* 2014) and, to some extent, the cementum layer of the teeth (Hansen *et al.* 2017) have increased the efficiency of experiments and the reliability of results, and have allowed some recent progress in retrieving ancient DNA information from difficult regions. Still, cultural factors such as cremation, the earliest East Asian example of which has been reported in Neolithic Jiangsu (Yan *et al.* 2022), and the prospect of selective burials (Fernández-Crespo & de-la-Rúa 2015) remind us that our understanding of the past through what remains has its own survivorship biases, and must be cautiously interpreted with an awareness that some records will be forever missing.

The genetic information recovered from fossil material consists of short sequences generated from fragments of DNA molecules which are likely to have acquired sequence-altering genetic lesions over the years. The most common of these is cytosine deamination (Briggs *et al.* 2007), or the conversion of cytosine to uracil, which manifests in recovered sequences as a conversion of cytosine to thymine. Protocols have been developed to remove or correct this damage using enzymatic or *in silico* approaches at various points along the chain of analysis (Briggs *et al.* 2010; Prüfer 2018; Rohland *et al.* 2015). Although the ubiquity of this form of damage decreases the reliability of these bases at lower coverages, this damage can serve a useful purpose in separating authentic ancient DNA from contaminating modern human DNA (Fu *et al.* 2015). Due to the low endogenous DNA content of ancient material, most common ancient genomics studies consider only an array of specific genomic loci, SNPs (single nucleotide polymorphisms), which have been predetermined to be informative between populations, such as the "Human Origins" SNP array consisting of approximately 600,000 SNPs (Patterson *et al.* 2012). The technique of targeted sequence capture (Ávila-Arcos *et al.* 2011; Fu *et al.* 2013) can increase the efficiency of ancient DNA recovery by targeting only those DNA fragments containing bases required for comparison between genomes. This approach uses synthetically created "bait" oligonucleotides to hybridize to ancient DNA fragments that contain sequences similar to those of the targeting baits, and is particularly useful when a high background of environmental DNA in a sample makes a non-targeted, "shotgun" sequencing approach infeasible.

Middle Pleistocene Archaic Humans

Archeological evidence attributes the earliest presence of archaic humans in East Asia to *Homo erectus*, the remains of which have been found in Yunnan Province and estimated to be 1.7 million years old ("Yuanmou 元谋 Man")

(Dong 2016), and a partial skull and mandible from Shaanxi province, estimated at 1.6 million years ago ("Lantian 蓝田 Man") (Zhu *et al.* 2015). These dates are slightly older than the earliest appearance of *Homo erectus* in Indonesia (Zaim *et al.* 2011), although stone tools from Lantian may indicate an East Asian presence extending over two million years ago (Zhu *et al.* 2018). Additional traces of *Homo erectus* in East Asia have been dated to 500,000–400,000 years ago (Zhao *et al.* 2001), and possibly as young as 230,000 years ago (Yang 2014), which is considerably older than the more recent 108,000-year-old remains attributed to *Homo erectus* found in the islands of Indonesia (Rizal *et al.* 2020). Although *Homo erectus* populations have successfully migrated from Africa to East Asia and were able to adapt and survive, at least during certain periods, for over one million years, researchers have yet to successfully recover DNA from any *Homo erectus* remains that could better inform us to the possible interactions between these populations and later archaic groups that have entered the region. The recovery of small fragments of ancient proteins from a 1.77-million-year-old *Homo erectus* tooth from Dmansi, Georgia, did not uncover enough information to allow a useful phylogenetic analysis (Welker *et al.* 2020). This study did, however, allow the placement of an 800,000-year-old *Homo antecessor* from Spain as a sister lineage, branching earlier from that which would give rise in the middle Pleistocene to *Homo sapiens*, Neanderthals, and Denisovans. For the moment, it appears that ancient proteomics, and not ancient genetics, will be the obligatory method to explore phylogenetic questions of super-archaic humans.

Traces of Neanderthals have yet to be found in East Asia; however, their remains and attributed artifacts have been uncovered in several caves in the foothills of the Altai mountain range in southern Siberia, marking the easternmost point of their distribution. Analysis of genetic material preserved in the sediments of Denisova Cave places the earliest appearance of Neanderthals there at approximately 195,000 years ago, at a time when the cave appears to have been also intermittently occupied by Denisovans (Zavala *et al.* 2021). Mitochondrial DNA fragments belonging to Neanderthal lineages have been recovered from all sedimentary layers bearing hominin DNA from Denisova Cave, dating their continued appearance until the earliest traces of modern human mitochondrial sequences around roughly 44,000 years ago, concurrent with the Initial Upper Paleolithic (IUP) technologies in the region. Apart from the periods between 120,000 and 97,000 years ago and after 49,000 years ago, all layers containing Neanderthal DNA also contained DNA from Denisovans, revealing that these two archaic populations likely lived with some awareness of each other, at least intermittently. Archeological and genetic evidence from Denisova, Chagyrskaya, and Okladnikov caves indicates that at least two successive populations of Neanderthals were present in the Altai Mountains over the 150,000-year span of their occupation (Kolobova *et al.* 2020; Zavala *et al.* 2021). In Denisova Cave sediments, Neanderthal mitochondrial sequence older than 150,000 years belonged to a more basal Neanderthal lineage, with younger sequences being similar to more recent Neanderthal lineages found in the Altai Mountains and western Europe (Zavala *et al.* 2021). The co-occurrence of DNA from both Neanderthal and Denisovan populations in the same sedimentary layers marks Denisova Cave as a point of overlapping ranges belonging to these two archaic populations. Genomic analysis of a 90,000-year-old bone fragment, which was determined to belong to a child of a Neanderthal mother and Denisovan father, provides evidence that these two populations occasionally interacted in southern Siberia (Slon *et al.* 2018).

Denisovan remains have been much more difficult to characterize than those of Neanderthals, primarily due to the lack of morphological information of this enigmatic population. To date, only a single phalanx (Bennett *et al.* 2019), a partial mandible (Chen *et al.* 2019), and several teeth (Reich *et al.* 2010) offer the only diagnostic morphological data; thus, the identification of Denisovan remains can only be reliably concluded based on molecular evidence. As their morphological characteristics become better understood, existing hominin material from East Asia, some of it taxonomically challenging, may eventually be classified as Denisovan. It has been alternatively suggested that two Neanderthal-like crania discovered in Henan, China (Li *et al.* 2017), as well as a new Homo species described on the island of Luzon in the Philippines (Détroit *et al.* 2019) may have possibly belonged to Denisovan populations (Teixeira *et al.* 2021), and several other Middle Pleistocene skulls with cryptic traits found between Yunnan to the south and Heilongjiang to the north of China have also been suggested as candidate Denisovan remains (Demeter *et al.* 2022). The answers will await the discovery of new material, or improved techniques to enhance the detection of ancient diagnostic amino acid or DNA sequences from existing East Asian archaic human remains.

The geographic range and population structure of Denisovans are largely unknown, although genetic studies of modern humans have given some tantalizing, if incongruous, hints. The hypoxia pathway gene *EPAS1*, which has been shown to regulate hemoglobin levels at high altitudes, was found to have introgressed into modern-day Tibetans through an ancient admixture with Denisovans, indicating a past selective pressure for high-altitude adaptations (Huerta-Sánchez *et al.* 2014). This fits well with the genetic and archeological evidence placing the Denisovan population range around the Tibetan Plateau and the Altai Mountains. However, the highest amount of Denisovan genetic ancestry among present-day populations is found among the islands of the

Philippines and Papua New Guinea (Larena *et al.* 2021a; Reich *et al.* 2011), much further away and at lower altitudes, raising many questions about the range and genetic diversity of these East Asian archaic humans. Deeper analysis into the Denisovan ancestry of modern humans has given insights as to the timing and probable locations of Denisovan introgression, and has identified separate admixture events between the ancestors of modern humans and several genetically distinct Denisovan populations. These events also show some geographic constraints, with a large proportion of the Denisovan ancestry restricted to modern Papuans being derived from a population more genetically distant from the Denisovans of the Altai Mountains that more closely match the lower levels of ancestry present in both East Asians and Papuans (Browning *et al.* 2018). A third Denisovan admixture event which is thought to have introduced the *EPAS1* allele into the ancestors of modern Tibetans appears to be from a population more closely related to the Altai Denisovan genome (Huerta-Sánchez *et al.* 2014). These three events were estimated to have occurred between 30,000 and 49,000 years ago, pointing to modern human and Denisovan interactions across a broad East Asian landscape occupied by different Denisovan populations. So far, only those inhabiting the Altai region have been genetically characterized from ancient DNA.

The earliest evidence anywhere of Denisovans can be traced to mitochondrial sequences in Denisova cave sediments, where they have been found within the oldest hominin DNA-bearing layers, as old as 250,000 years ago. These results also showed Denisovan occupancy in this cave to have lasted at least until 55,000 years ago (Zavala *et al.* 2021). Hominin hand and footprints, circumstantially assigned to Denisovans and dating to as old as 226,000 years ago, have been described 2,300 km away from Denisova Cave in the Tibetan plateau, at an elevation of over 4,000 meters (Zhang *et al.* 2021a). A 160,000-year-old mandible from Baishiya Karst Cave 白石崖溶洞 in Gansu, China, has been characterized as likely to be Denisovan through ancient protein sequencing (Chen *et al.* 2019). Although the DNA was too poorly preserved to recover genetic information from it, this sample may represent the first Denisovan material found outside of Denisova Cave. As has been done in Denisova Cave, greater details of the Denisovan occupation of Baishiya cave were learned through Denisovan DNA recovered through a cross section of the sediment, offering the first genetic proof of Denisovan presence on the Tibetan plateau and unequivocally extending the known range of Denisovans (Zhang *et al.* 2020). Unlike in the Altai region, Baishiya cave appears to have been inhabited exclusively by Denisovans, since no Neanderthal DNA was detected in any layer. At least two occupation periods were proposed, an earlier one at approximately 100,000 years ago, and a more recent one between 60,000 and possibly 45,000 years ago. It is clear that the true age range of the Denisovan presence in Baishiya Cave may not be determined from sediments alone, since both of these dates are considerably younger than the proposed Denisovan mandible that had been found there (Zhang *et al.* 2020). Phylogenetic analysis of the mitochondrial sequences recovered from the sediment showed the more recent Baishiya Cave occupants, dating from 60,000 years ago, to be genetically similar to the relatively contemporary Denisovan occupants of Denisova Cave (Denisova3 and Denisova4), whereas older occupational levels at both sites contained more deeply branching Denisovan mitochondrial sequences. The sequence differences between the younger and older Denisovan inhabitants of Denisova Cave indicate a split time of the two populations that may have been greater than 200,000 years ago (Zavala *et al.* 2021). These results imply a broad population turnover event at some point after 80,000 years ago where Denisovan inhabitants of the Tibetan Plateau and Altai region were replaced by a more recently diverged population. One possible origin of this replacing population may have been from the southeast along the eastern Himalayan foothills, traveling to the Altai region along with other migrant fauna appearing in the Altai during the Pleistocene (Agadjanian & Shunkov 2018). This incoming population would have necessarily been genetically distinct from southern Asian Denisovan populations found to have admixed with Papuans, which may have been located in Southeast Asia or among islands of Wallacea or the Philippines. They may also have originated elsewhere in China, but ancient genetic information from either of these regions is still missing. This highlights the large gap in our knowledge regarding the geographic distribution and genetic characteristics of other Denisovan populations. Fossil material for these southern populations has yet to be found or convincingly identified through molecular analysis. The recent discovery of a possibly 150,000-year-old molar from Tam Ngu Hao 2 Cave in Laos bearing Denisovan morphological characteristics may represent one of these mysterious southern Denisovan populations (Demeter *et al.* 2022), although high temperatures and humid climates in these regions make the adequate preservation of molecular evidence from this time period difficult. Further discoveries and research will be needed to expand our knowledge of Denisovan population structure and dynamics and the impact these populations had on modern human diversity.

The Earliest Modern Humans in East Asia

The question of the first arrival of modern humans into East Asia has been fraught with sometimes conflicting genetic and archeological evidence. Modern genomic studies support a model whereby all non-Africans descended from populations that began leaving the African continent at some point after roughly 65,000 years ago. The appearance of anatomically modern human remains in several caves in southern China below U-series dated flowstones suggesting dates up to 120,000 years old has been used to argue a possible arrival along the southern Eurasian coast pre-dating this initial out-of-Africa event (Bae *et al.* 2014; Liu *et al.* 2015; Shen *et al.* 2013). Recent work, however, has shown water circulation can transport the sedimentary material collected beneath flowstones, and in fact none of this supposedly older material has been radiocarbon-dated to earlier than 30,000 years (Sun *et al.* 2021). Current data supports a date of modern human entry into East Asia as no earlier than 55,000 to 50,000 years ago (Hublin 2021). Additionally, a recent genomic study of several 45,000-year-old modern humans in Bacho Kiro Cave in eastern Europe has found these individuals to be genetically closer to modern humans found in East Asia than to those in Europe (Hajdinjak *et al.* 2021). The oldest ancestry similar to that found in modern Europeans does not appear in Europe until at least 37,000 years ago (Seguin-Orlando *et al.* 2014). This observation suggests that the inhabitants of East Asia may be more closely related to the initial migration waves of modern humans that first populated Eurasia. If earlier groups had arrived in East Asia prior to this successful migration, they appear to have left no surviving descendants.

The obstacle of the Himalayan Mountain range appears to have restricted the earliest entries into East Asia into northern and southern routes. Although the details are far from settled, ancient and modern genomic studies appear to favor a southern route into East Asia for the majority of genetic diversity present there today. This is based primarily on the East Asian basal population branching closely with southern Eurasian lineages leading to Australians, Papuans, and the more deeply branching Andaman Islanders (Larena *et al.* 2021b; Lipson & Reich 2017). This structure describes a general model of groups expanding along the southern part of the Asian continent and sequentially separating into genetically distinct populations. It is important to note that the 40,000-year-old Tianyuan individual found in northern China near Beijing can be genetically modeled as basal to both northern and southern East Asian lineages (Fu *et al.* 2013; Yang *et al.* 2017), giving a minimal timeframe of the arrival of this ancestry in to northern East Asia.

An IUP Industry coinciding with some of the earliest appearance of modern humans in western Eurasia has also been described in Central Asia and Siberia, with its easternmost appearance in Northwest China (Zwyns 2021). Early appearances of IUP artifacts have been reported in Denisova Cave (Douka *et al.* 2019) and the 45,000-year-old Tolbor-16 site in northern Mongolia

(Zwyns *et al.* 2019) which are similar archeologically to a 41,000-year-old site in Shuidonggou 水洞沟, China (Peng *et al.* 2020). These findings raise the possibility of a dispersal of modern humans bearing IUP lithic traditions into East Asia along a northern inland route through northern or Central Asia and southeast from Siberia (Li *et al.* 2019), possibly facilitated by the Greenland Interstadial 12 temperate climatic period beginning roughly 47,000 years ago (Rasmussen *et al.* 2014). To date however, no genetic material associated with these sites has been recovered that can inform us as to which human populations they belonged. A genome from a 45,000-year-old modern human from western Siberia known as Ust' Ishim represented a population with no present-day surviving ancestry that descended from a population ancestral to both eastern and western Eurasians near a time when these populations were becoming distinct from each other, and earlier than the split of the lineage leading to Tianyuan (Fu *et al.* 2014; Vallini *et al.* 2022). If these East Asian IUP sites were to be linked to populations related to Ust' Ishim it would appear these people left no detectable genetic legacy in modern East Asia. It may also be found that the material at some of these IUP sites was created by populations derived from East Asian lineages linked to or branching from Tianyuan, or a western Eurasian ancestry lineage present later in the northern Siberian Mid Upper Paleolithic (Sikora *et al.* 2019), or some yet undiscovered ancestry. An additional potentially modern human Late Pleistocene lithic site in East Asia, Nwya Devu 尼阿底, has been reported on the Tibetan Plateau dating up to 40,000 years ago and bearing similarities to the IUP industry of Shuidonggou (Zhang *et al.* 2018). At 4,600 meters above sea level, this is the highest altitude Upper Pleistocene site yet found. Although no human remains have been found there, the proximity of this site to Tibetan Denisovan populations, such as those present at Baishiya Cave, may have allowed an opportunity for the introgression of the Denisovan *EPAS1* hypoxia reducing allele that would have facilitated modern human occupation at this altitude. The genomic characterization of the people behind these East Asian IUP archeological sites will be an important step in better understanding the migration routes and population dynamics of modern humans entering East Asia.

Overview of Ancient East Asian Modern Human Populations

The recent increased focus in ancient East Asian genomes has uncovered a complex distribution of regional ancestries that can be used to discern the migrations of modern humans into East Asia and their subsequent movements and interactions over the past several thousands of years. In many cases, these lineages can be traced to a basal East Asian lineage referred to as East- and

Southeast Asian (ESEA) (Yang 2022), which is ancestral to most of the groups currently living in East and Southeast Asia. The broad clade of ESEA ancestry includes Austronesian ancestry found in Polynesia, as well as the basal Upper Paleolithic Tianyuan individual from northern China. Sister groups to the ESEA lineage include the earlier branching Australasians (AA), which includes modern-day Papuans, Aboriginal Australians and inhabitants of neighboring islands, and the Ancient Ancestral South Indian (AASI) lineage, a branch of South Asian hunter-gatherer ancestry which contributed to groups found primarily in present-day southern India, although it is also found in low levels throughout South Asia (Narasimhan *et al.* 2019). Andaman Islanders (represented by the present-day Önge population) belong to a deeply branching lineage of the East Asian expansion possibly branching early in the AA lineage but also containing some genetic similarities to AASI ancestry (Narasimhan *et al.* 2019) (Figure 1). The presence of Önge-related ancestry in many ESEA groups along the coast of China and Paleolithic Japan, but not in ancient interior populations, has been proposed as a signal of a coastal route of human migration into East Asia (Wang *et al.* 2021a). More information about the timing and directionality of this deeply branching signal could better resolve its origin.

The dominant lineage found in East Asia, ESEA, has been further subdivided through ongoing ancient genomics research into regional ancestries, usually named for where they were first detected, although settlement patterns and later population movements often ensure ancestries do not fit neatly within regional borders for all time periods. The East Asian regions this Element will focus on cover the expanse of the modern borders of China, Mongolia, Japan, and Korea, from the Amur and West Liao River region in the northeast, where some of the oldest East Asian populations have been characterized, to the southern areas of Guangxi, containing a deeply branching lost lineage, and Fujian, home of the ancestors of the Pacific-faring Austronesians. We will then turn to the early millet farmers along the Yellow River, moving from the lower reaches of Shandong, through Henan, and into the northern inland regions of the Loess Plateau. To the west, we will summarize our current knowledge of the origins of Tibetan populations and the population structures of Xinjiang and neighboring Mongolia since the Bronze Age, and, finally, to the east we will discuss the emerging understanding of the peopling of Japan and the Korean peninsula. Although much has been learned through the recent analysis of ancient populations in these regions, many crucial puzzle pieces are still missing, notably the Yangtze River Basin, where rice cultivation may have first occurred, still awaits in-depth study, and the genetic interrelationships of many important East Asian prehistoric populations and cultures still remain to be investigated.

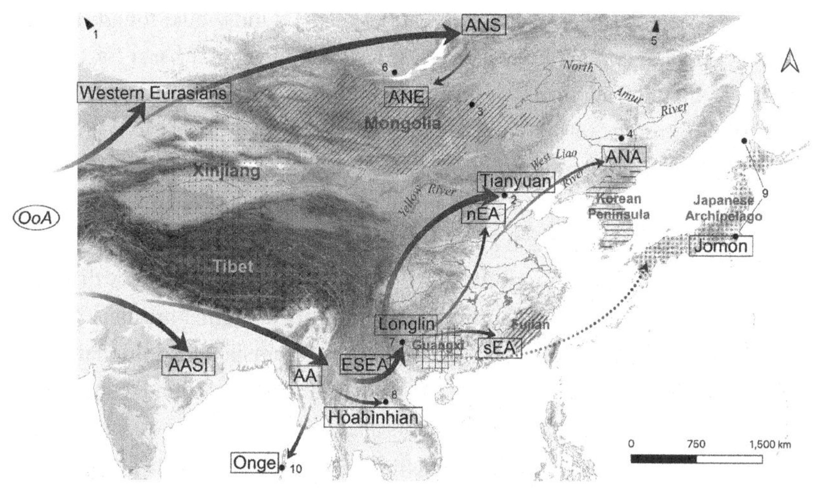

Figure 1 The proposed branching sequences of the primary ancestral lineages of East Asia (in boxes) discussed in the text with their approximate geographic locations. Arrows show possible movements and do not suggest actual routes. The route by which the Jōmon arrived to the Japanese Archipelago (dotted line) has yet to be determined. Textured patterns surrounding gray labels define the regions featured in sections of the text. AA = Australasian, AASI = Ancient Ancestral South Indian, ANA = Ancient Northeastern Asian, ANE = Ancient Northern Eurasian, ANS = Ancient Northern Siberian, ESEA = East and Southeast Asian, nEA = northern East Asian, OoA = Out of Africa, sEA = southern East Asian. Numbered dots indicate locations of ancient individuals with key ancestries and their approximate age, as the rounded date given in the source publication (in BP). 1, Ust'-Ishim (45 k); 2, Tianyuan (40 k); 3, Salkhit (34 k); 4, AR33K (33 k); 5, Yana (32 k); 6, Mal'ta (24 k); 7, Longlin ("ancient Guangxi," 11 k); 8, Hòabìnhian (8 k); 9, Jōmon (3 k); 10, Önge (present-day).

Northeastern East Asia

Although geographically distant from the major presumed entry points into the region, the northeastern parts of East Asia contain some of the oldest modern humans who have been genetically characterized in Eastern Eurasia. The region borders Siberia to the north and includes the Amur River Basin, which spans Siberia, Mongolia and northeastern China, and the West Liao River to the West. The Amur River forms the natural border between China and Siberia and contains the Songhua 松花 and Nen 嫩 River tributaries. The genomes of human remains recovered along this broad alluvial plain were analyzed in a deep time transect study spanning over 30,000 years of occupation. It was determined that the oldest of these, a 33,000-year-old individual found without any archeological context known as AR33K, shared a similar basal East Asian ancestry to that of Tianyuan, who lived 1,100 km to the southwest 7,000 years earlier (Mao *et al.* 2021). To date, this Tianyuan-like ancestry is the sole ancestry found to be present in northeastern East Asia prior to the Last Glacial Maximum (LGM). In northern Siberia, nearly 3,000 km from where AR33K was discovered, slightly younger genomes recovered from two children at a 32,000-year-old habitation site by the Yana River, described a very different ancestry that had split from the lineage leading to western Eurasians 4,000–5,000 years after separating from that of eastern Eurasians. Additionally, the western Eurasian ancestry present at the Yana River site was found to have later received an early influx of about 20% of its ancestry from an East Asian lineage. The ancestry at Yana was called Ancient North Siberian ancestry (ANS) and would play an important genetic role in later Siberian populations and to the groups that would colonize the Americas (Sikora *et al.* 2019). At a roughly contemporary site in the Salkhit Valley in northeastern Mongolia, a skull fragment also had admixed ancestry, sharing 75% with Tianyuan and 25% related to ANS ancestry (Massilani *et al.* 2020). These findings show that at least two divergent populations had established themselves in northeastern Eurasia during the Upper Paleolithic, ANS in Siberia and Tianyuan-related in northeastern China, and the evidence of their interactions was seen in the 34,000-year-old individual from Mongolia. Given the broad time difference between Tianyuan and AR33K and the distance between them, it is believed that Tianyuan-like ancestry was widespread throughout northeastern China, lasting at least until the Mid Upper Paleolithic.

There is no more population information available from this region until the close of the LGM, when the population profile of northeastern East Asia appears to have shifted. The Tianyuan genetic cluster disappears from the record, and not far from where AR33K lived near the Songua River, remains from a 19,000-year-old individual, AR19K, were identified instead to be more closely related to present-day East Asians. AR19K, who was also found without any archeological context, lived at the last years of the LGM when warming temperatures were beginning to return to what was still a cold steppe environment of northern East Asia, yet it is currently unclear when the AR19K-related population first migrated to the area, or when Tianyuan ancestry vanished, and what role the severe climatic and environmental changes of the LGM played in this population replacement. Several statistical models show that AR19K ancestry is basal to younger ancestries found throughout ancient coastal northern East Asia, and also that AR19K clusters more closely to ancient coastal northern East Asia populations than to ancient coastal southern East Asian ancestry (Mao *et al.*

2021). This prominent genetic distinction between northern and southern East Asian populations had been observed earlier with younger samples (Yang *et al.* 2020), but these results indicate that by 19,000 years ago this population structure was already in place.

The *EDAR* Variant

An adaptive genetic variant of the *EDAR* gene occurred in the ancestors of East Asian and Native American populations, where it has risen through positive selection to high frequencies in these groups (Kamberov *et al.* 2013), with an average 91.6% frequency among several East Asian populations. The variant, *EDAR_V370A*, codes for a cell surface receptor related to ectodermal development resulting in a phenotype of shovel-shaped incisors, thick hair shafts, and increased sweat glands (Bryk *et al.* 2008). There have been several theories as to the specific selective pressure through which positive selection had acted on this variant, and where and when this process began, but the answers have yet to be satisfactorily determined. Age estimates for this mutation using various models have been between 3,000 and 22,000 years ago, and possibly as old as 43,000 (Bryk *et al.* 2008; Peter *et al.* 2012; Smith *et al.* 2018). Suggested selective advantages have considered that the allele may have increased vitamin-D intake from milk in low UV environments during the LGM 23,000 years ago, or alternatively, the allele may have aided heat dispersal during a warm period of high humidity beginning 40,000 years ago (Kamberov *et al.* 2013). The oldest individual yet identified with the *EDAR_V370A* variant has been AR19K in the Amur Region, which places the allele at the latest toward the end of the LGM. It is common in subsequent northeastern East Asia individuals but absent in pre-LGM AR33K and Tianyuan (Mao *et al.* 2021). It has also been reported to be absent in ancient Jōmon individuals and Papuans (Wang *et al.* 2021a). More information is needed to better understand the origin and selective advantages of this variant, but current data suggest the allele originated along an inland East Asian lineage, perhaps during the LGM, which would imply selective pressure occurred during a challenging cold climatic period.

Ancient Northeast Asian Ancestry

Several Neolithic groups around the Amur River Basin dating from between 14,000 and 2,000 years ago have been analyzed genetically and have been found to cluster together with a common ancestry described as Ancient Northeast Asian (ANA) (Mao *et al.* 2021; Ning *et al.* 2020b; Robbeets *et al.* 2021; Siska *et al.* 2017; Wang *et al.* 2021a). ANA ancestry could be modeled as branching from a common lineage as that of AR19K, although with some genetic distance separating these two ancestries (Mao *et al.* 2021). ANA ancestry has been found in Neolithic hunter-gatherer populations living in the Amur region and Primorye to the east, as well as Baikal in Siberia, the Inner Mongolian Plateau, and the West Liao River. During the Neolithic it was present at the Songhua River, the Houtaomuga 后套木嘎 site near Da'an 大安 in Jilin province of China, the site of Jalainur 扎赉诺尔 in eastern Inner Mongolian, as well as the coastal populations of Devil's Gate Cave (Chertovy Vorota) and the Boisman-2 site in the Primorye region of Siberia, and appears to have been indigenous to these regions since at least the Paleolithic era. These and other contemporary sites in northeast East Asia containing relevant archeological material indicate that these groups practiced a hunter-gatherer subsistence strategy supplemented by intensified fishing and limited horticulture (Kuzmin 2013), but did not practice large-scale organized agriculture at this time. In contrast to the common interpretation of the Neolithic of Europe, the Neolithic of eastern Eurasia is marked not by the beginning of structured farming practices but by a broader spectrum of human behavioral changes including the appearance of pottery, where it predated the Holocene (Popov *et al.* 2014). In northern East Asia, pottery has been documented more than 14,000 years ago (Kuzmin 2017; Shoda *et al.* 2020), while organized millet cultivation does not appear in the Amur River Valley until after 6,000 years ago (Li *et al.* 2020). An additional east-west genetic cline has been reported for ANA populations, with higher similarity to Neolithic Mongolians to the west and higher ancestry related to Jōmon 绳文 populations from Paleolithic Japan to the east (Robbeets *et al.* 2021).

Compared to present-day populations, ANA ancestry is most similar to Tungusic and Nivkh language speakers such as the Ulchi, Oroqen, Hazhen, and Nivkh, all of whom still live in the same geographic region as the Neolithic ANA populations (Ning *et al.* 2020b), and thus represent a genetic and geographic continuity going back at least 14,000 years. Possible reasons for the persistence of ANA populations for so long may have been related to the late adoption of agriculture, having not arrived in the Amur Region until the Middle to Late Neolithic (Cui *et al.* 2020). The difficulty of transferring agriculture from warmer to colder climates and the reliance on alternative food sources may have protected this region from the severe regional climatic variations that can impact agriculture-based societies (Lutaenko *et al.* 2007) and helped them to resist population expansions from the south tied to the spread of agriculture (Mao *et al.* 2021; Ning *et al.* 2020b). A steady decrease in genetic relatedness in the Amur Region over the Neolithic period as measured by Runs of Homozygosity analysis, which can be used to derive population demography and size by looking at the length of identical genomic sections, has been linked to an expanding population indicative of a continuous successful exploitation of the resources of the area (Mao *et al.* 2021).

West Liao River Farmers and the Origins of the Transeurasian Language Family

The West Liao River flows from its tributaries in the steppes of the Inner Mongolian Plateau where it joins the East Liao River and continues into the Liaodong 辽东 Bay in the Yellow Sea. Unlike the Neolithic subsistence practices of the Amur region to the northeast, the Hongshan 红山 culture in the West Liao River valley had been cultivating Broomcorn millet as a staple crop by the Middle Neolithic, beginning 6,500 years ago (Li *et al.* 2020; Sun & Zhao 2013). Several genetic studies of these early farmers in the West Liao River region have concluded both Middle Neolithic Hongshan and Early Bronze Age Lower Xiajiadian cultures of the West Liao River contained ANA ancestry mixed with ancestry from farming societies found along the Yellow River to the south in Shandong and Henan, and associated with the Neolithic Longshan 龙山 culture (Ning *et al.* 2020b). The cultural transition from the Lower to the Upper Xiajiadian 夏家店 beginning roughly 3,000 years ago saw the trend reverse, and an increase in ANA ancestry over Yellow River ancestry (YR) occurred. This population shift coincided with mid-Holocene climatic changes to a colder, dryer period at the end of the Holocene Optimum and the adoption of a more pastoral lifestyle around the West Liao River, which appears to have been related to population expansions from the north (Jia *et al.* 2016; Ning *et al.* 2020b).

Transeurasian Language Dispersal

The discovery that ANA ancestry is carried by all present-day speakers of Transeurasian languages, a macro-family largely encompassing the proto-languages of Mongolic, Turkic, Tungusic, Koreanic, and Japonic, has led to genetic and multidisciplinary investigations of the origins of the Transeurasian language family (Ning *et al.* 2020b; Robbeets *et al.* 2021; Wang *et al.* 2021a). These studies leverage information of the dispersal of ancient genetic ancestral components to test the validity of the Transeurasian hypothesis, which posits that these language groups arose from a proto-language that expanded from the West Liao River Basin along with the spread of millet farmers during the Neolithic. There has been substantial geographical and temporal overlap found between ANA ancestry and the linguistic histories of these languages. Some of these results agree with an Early Neolithic eastward movement of separate West Liao River populations into Primorye and Korea, which may correspond to the proto-Altaic and proto-Japano-Koreanic, language groups, respectively, the second group being linked to admixed ANA and YR ancestry. Bronze Age migrations corresponding to the Upper Xiajiadian-related ancestry arrived in Japan from Liaodong via the Korean Penninsula bearing an expanded agricultural package including rice, barley, and wheat. The westward spread from West Liao River populations into the eastern Eurasian Steppes during the Bronze Age, where they admixed with arriving western Eurasian ancestry, may account for noted linguistic borrowings concerning agriculture and pastoralism found in proto-Mongolic and proto-Turkic language groups (Robbeets *et al.* 2021). One complication of these findings is that in addition to ANA, the earliest genomes from the West Liao River also contain YR ancestry, which is not found in Amur or Primorye (Ning *et al.* 2020b). It has been argued that the West Liao River genomes that have been characterized so far date only to the Middle Neolithic, and older genomes from this region should predate these YR ancestry admixture events (Robbeets *et al.* 2021). Another complication is that the similarities between Neolithic ANA ancestries originating from the West Liao River with those native to the Amur region make such movements into this region difficult to track genetically.

Contributions to Native Americans

The exploration of the genetic history of northern East Asia has also had a major impact in our understanding of the origins of Native American groups. A 10,000-year-old genome from a site near the Kolyma River in northeastern Siberia was found to contain a distinct genetic ancestry, Ancient Paleo-Siberian (APS) (Sikora *et al.* 2019), which can be modeled as an admixture between west Eurasian branching ANS-like ancestry, such as that found in Yana, and an East Asian lineage. Although it was known that Ancient North Eurasian (ANE) ancestry, such as that of the 25,000-year-old MA-1 individual from Mal'ta near Lake Baikal in Siberia, shared ancestry with Native Americans, it was clear that ANE ancestry required additional East Asian gene flow in order to approximate the Native American founding population (Moreno-Mayar *et al.* 2018; Raghavan *et al.* 2014). APS ancestry found in Kolyma1 was the closest match to this founding population, as represented by genomes recovered from two children at the 11,500-year-old Alaskan site Upward Sun River in North America, USR1 (Moreno-Mayar *et al.* 2018), yet in attempts to best model the relationship between APS ancestry and USR1 using statistical genetics, Kolyma1 still lacked additional ancestry from an unidentified East Asian source. Among the currently available ancient sources, AR14K from the Amur Region was determined to be the closest candidate to this East Asian source, permitting the Native American USR1 to be modeled as an admixture of 20–30% AR14K-related East Asian ancestry and 70–80% APS ancestry (Mao *et al.* 2021). Demographic models estimate the split between APS and populations ancestral to Native Americans to have occurred approximately 24,000 years ago (Sikora *et al.* 2019). Other interpretations have questioned the simple model of a single early founding population and propose several migration waves across Beringia with different levels of ANA ancestry (Ning *et al.* 2020a). Additional research and samples will be needed to better identify potential source populations closer to these separation events, and the areas where they were likely to have occurred, as well as to determine the complex population dynamics of Upper Paleolithic northeast Eurasia and Beringia with relation to Native American founding groups.

Southern East Asia

In contrast to the details we have of the first arrival of modern humans in northern East Asia, the story of the Upper Paleolithic in southern East Asia, covering Fujian and Taiwan on the southern Chinese coast and areas laterally westward to the borders of Southeast Asia, is much less clear. Efforts to resolve this period are impeded by the warm and wet climate of southern East Asia that is much less likely to preserve both organic material and DNA. Several samples dating to the Early Neolithic have been analyzed along the southeastern coast of Fujian and inland at Guangxi and indicate a complex demographic history of southern East Asian populations involving both isolation and admixture among them and with more distant groups. Combined with archeological results, the picture emerging is one of early cultural contacts between southern East Asia, Southeast Asia, and coastal northern East Asia groups (Matsumura & Oxenham 2014; Stoneking & Delfin 2010; Wang *et al.* 2021a, 2021b). Such complexity might be expected as southern East Asia remains a genetic and cultural mosaic containing five linguistic families, Austroasiatic, Austronesian, Daic, Hmong-Mien, and Sino-Tibetan. Admixture models indicate the principal ancestry of southern East Asia during this period belonged to an East Asian lineage more closely related to other contemporary groups from northern East Asia rather than to the older Tianyuan and AR33K (McColl *et al.* 2018; Wang *et al.* 2021b; Yang *et al.* 2020). This indicates that Early Neolithic southern East Asians and those appearing in northern East Asia after the LGM split more recently from each other than either group did with the Upper Paleolithic Tianyuan-related group. As mentioned earlier, the north-south genetic cline of East Asia had already been in place at the close of the LGM, and this is also seen in the genomes of Early Neolithic southern East Asians (Yang *et al.* 2020).

Previously, a "two-layer" model had been proposed to explain human migration and interactions across East and Southeast Asia based on cranial morphometrics and dental characteristics (Matsumura *et al.* 2019). In this model, the first layer represents hunter-gatherers based on distinctive skeletal features, which were largely replaced by a second layer population, having skeletal characteristics more common in present-day East and Southeast Asians and associated with the practice of agriculture, extended position burials, and material related to the Neolithic package. Based on this hypothesis, first-layer populations should show very little genetic contribution to people belonging to the second layer. However, recent ancient DNA studies contradict the past morphological studies (Lipson *et al.* 2018; McColl *et al.* 2018; Wang *et al.* 2021b), and both East Asian farmers and indigenous hunter-gatherers contributed to genetic the diversity of present-day southern East and Southeast Asians. Southern East Asians dating to 12,000–8,000 years ago that exhibit first-layer cranial morphologies are closely related genetically to presumed second-layer East Asian populations, demonstrating that demographic models based solely on morphology are not sufficient to describe the population movement, replacement, and admixture in post-LGM East Asia (Lipson *et al.* 2018; McColl *et al.* 2018; Wang *et al.* 2021b; Yang *et al.* 2020).

Fujian Coastal Populations

Fujian is a mountainous province located in southeastern China along the coast of the East China Sea that contains a narrow, low, coastal plain facing the island of Taiwan across the Taiwan Strait. The Fujian coast is characterized by numerous small islands, including Liangdao 亮岛, where 8,300-year-old remains were recovered beneath a shell mound containing pottery and tools made from both stone and bone. Genomic analysis of the individual, Liangdao1, along with Liangdao2, a second individual who lived approximately 600 years later, found they clustered closely together with two individuals who were excavated from the Qihe 奇和 cave site in mainland Fujian, an 8,400-year-old individual, Qihe2, and a 12,000-year-old Qihe3. This ancient southern coastal East Asian ancestry, later termed ancient Fujian ancestry, had close genetic similarities to Neolithic Southeast Asians and Austronesian-related islanders from the Southwest Pacific, and have all been shown in statistical tests to share more similarities with each other than with northern ancient East Asian groups (Wang *et al.* 2021b; Yang *et al.* 2020).

In the Late Neolithic, the Tanshishan 昙石山 culture arose after 5,000 years ago in the lower Min River 岷江 valley in Fujian. The Tanshishan site shows evidence of mixed rice and millet farming from at least 5,000 years ago

(Dai *et al.* 2021), and the culture shared characteristics with the Longshan culture in the Yellow River valley (Chang 1989 p. 89). To characterize the long-term demographic changes of the southeastern Chinese coastal populations, 4,500-year-old populations from two Tanshishan sites, Tanshishan and Xitoucun 溪头村, were investigated along with the contemporary site of Suogang 锁港 on the southeastern coast of the Penghu 澎湖 archipelago in the Taiwan Strait. These younger southeastern coastal East Asia populations also clustered with the older Fujian ancestry from the Early Neolithic, showing the persistence of the regional populations for over 8,000 years, however these southern populations were not equally differentiated from coastal and inland populations from northern East Asia. Some Late Neolithic Fujian (Fujian_LN) ancestry was genetically closer to Early Neolithic northern coastal East Asians than to inland groups, a pattern less pronounced but still observed in Early Neolithic Fujian (Fujian_EN) ancestry (Yang *et al.* 2020). These connections, which are also supported by maternal genetics (Liu *et al.* 2021), could be described by increasing gene flow between coastal populations, although some deeper population structure cannot also be ruled out.

Austronesians

Cultural links have been previously noted between Neolithic southern mainland coastal populations and the Austronesian groups who populated Taiwan 6,000 years ago (Wu 2021). Austronesians would later colonize islands of the South West Pacific and Indian Oceans beginning some 2,000 years later, eventually reaching as far as the African coast and distant islands of the Pacific, but their mainland origins have been difficult to identify. Three models have been proposed for the origin of the Neolithic in Taiwan: (1) the Mainland East Asian Interaction Sphere proposes a local expansion of the mainland Neolithic across the Taiwan strait and is supported by similarities in pre-agriculture ceramics; (2) the Northeastern Seaboard theory describes an origin from the coast of northeastern China, especially around the Shandong Peninsula, and is supported by a proposed Sino-Tibetan linguistic origin of Austronesian languages (Sagart *et al.* 2005); and (3) a Lower Yangtze (LY) origin from the expansion of Hemudu 河姆渡 culture-linked rice agriculturalists along the lower Yangtze River Basin (Sagart *et al.* 2018).

Ancient genomic studies can shed light on this debate by directly comparing early Austronesians with their ancient potential source populations. In doing this, several 3,000-year-old Austronesian-related southwestern Pacific Islanders from Vanuatu (Skoglund *et al.* 2016) were found to be a sister group to Fujian_LN populations from the southern East Asian mainland (Yang *et al.* 2020). This signal is obscured when comparing the ancient Austronesians to present-day and even contemporary southern East Asian populations due to an elevated proportion of northern East Asian ancestry in Fujian, a continuation of a trend already observed in the Neolithic. From Taiwan, 3,000- to 1,000-year-old Austronesians (Ko *et al.* 2014) also have been found to contain some northern ancestry, and can be modeled as having approximately 25% ancient northern East Asian ancestry similar to that found in the West Liao or Yellow Rivers, near Shandong (nEA, described herein), and 75% southern East Asian ancestry matching Fujian_EN, as represented by the 8,300-year-old remains from Liangdao, an ancestry also present in Tai-Kadai, Austroasiatic, and Austronesian language speakers (Wang *et al.* 2021a). The presence of northern East Asian ancestry makes the sequenced Austronesian genomes from Taiwan poor sources for the ancient southwest Pacific Austronesians who lack this northern component, but the relationship to mainland groups becomes clearer with the Neolithic data from the mainland. Additionally, both Fujian_EN and _LN share more alleles with present-day indegenous groups from Taiwan than with other present-day southern East Asian groups (Yang *et al.* 2020). Mitochondrial sequences also support this relationship. The mitochondrial haplogroup, E, recovered from Liangdao1 is rare in present-day mainland East Asia, but is found at high frequencies among Austronesian language speakers. The Liangdao mitochondrial sequence occupies a position basal to those found in indigenous Atayal and Ami groups in Taiwan (Ko *et al.* 2014). Altogether, the shared ancestry between ancient Fujian populations and ancient Vanuatu, as well as the gene flow shared with populations in Taiwan, points to a geographic origin of Austronesians somewhere along the southern coast of China, although a specific population of the proto-Austronesians that can be modeled as their direct ancestors has not yet been found. These results appear to favor perhaps a combination of Mainland East Asian Interaction Sphere, and, depending on the date of appearance of northern East Asian component, the Northeastern Seaboard model, but Neolithic Yangtze populations have yet to be fully examined genetically, and future work may uncover additional connections.

Ancient Guangxi Ancestry and Admixture

Guangxi Province, characterized by a mountainous, karst topography and numerous caves, is located in southern China where it borders Vietnam and the Gulf of Tonkin. A 1979 excavation at Laomocao 老磨槽 Cave in Longlin 隆林 County, Guangxi, uncovered human remains including an unusually shaped skull that combined both archaic and modern features. Originally proposed to have belonged to a late-surviving archaic population, the skull was radiocarbon dated to only 11,000 years old. Despite its appearance, the genetic ancestry of the Longlin skull was found, however, to fall completely within modern human variation (Wang *et al.* 2021b). Characterizing the ancestry present in ancient Guangxi represented by Longlin was a challenge. Both Northern and Southern Neolithic East Asians shared more ancestry with each other than either did with Longlin, yet compared to more deeply branching East Asian lineages, such as Tianyuan, Papuans, Andaman Islanders, and a deeply diverged ancestry found in an 8,000-year-old hunter-gatherer from Southeast Asia, Hòabìnhian (McColl *et al.* 2018), Longlin was genetically closer to both northern and southern East Asian groups. This suggested the ancestry found in Longlin Cave, termed ancient Guangxi ancestry, represented a previously uncharacterized deeply branching East Asian lineage (Wang *et al.* 2021b) (Figure 1). The coalescence time of the mitochondrial haplogroup identified in Longlin, M71d, and the geographic distribution of related lineages, suggested a possible early migration between southern East Asia and mainland Southeast Asia by at least 22,000 years ago. Interestingly, ancient Guangxi ancestry shares a closer genetic relationship with the Paleolithic Jōmon in Japan than with either of the two major language groups found in present-day Guangxi, Tai-Kadai, and Hmong-Mien. Jōmon and ancient Guangxi ancestry are both similarly related to both northern and southern branches of mainland East Asian ancestry, which is indicative of a similar separation time, yet each shares different specific relationships with members of these groups. Jōmon and Guangxi ancestry thus appear to have separated early from the common East Asian ancestry prior to the diversification of the widespread northern and southern East Asian lineages, but some additional complexity among them remains to be clarified before the history of these two deeply branching ancestries can be more fully reconstructed (Wang *et al.* 2021b).

Ancient Guangxi ancestry seems to have left no descendants among modern populations, but a 9,000-year-old individual found in Dushan 独山 Cave, 400 kilometers from Longlin Cave, could be modeled as having 83% ancestry similar to ancient Fujian and a 17% ancestral contribution from a Longlin-related population, showing that ancient Guangxi ancestry persisted in the area in admixed form into at least the Early Neolithic. This could be explained by incoming groups related to southern coastal populations in Fujian mixing with, rather than completely replacing, an indigenous Guangxi population at some point prior to 9,000 years ago. Further analysis showed the ancient Fujian component of Dushan to be more closely derived from Fujian_LN populations such as Tanshishan, and even 2,000-year-old Taiwan islanders, than to older Fujian_EN populations such as Qihe and Liangdao (Wang *et al.* 2021b). The admixed Fujian-Guangxi ancestry of Dushan was also identified in two related individuals from Baojianshan 宝剑山 Cave near the Vietnam border dating from between 8,300 and 6,400 years ago. The Baojianshan ancestry, however, had an additional Southeast Asian element not seen before in East Asia, and could be modeled as 72% Dushan-related ancestry and 28% ancestry similar to Hòabìnhian (Wang *et al.* 2021b). Hòabìnhian ancestry was first identified from remains associated with the Hòabìnhian Cultural complex in Laos and Malaysia, the examples of which are mainly concentrated in mainland Southeast Asia, where Hòabìnhian ancestry has been presumed to represent indigenous Southeast Asian hunter-gatherer groups. Hòabìnhian ancestry is also closely associated with present-day groups speaking Austroasiatic languages (McColl *et al.* 2018) (Figure 1). The findings from Baojianshan expand the range of groups carrying Southeast Asian Hòabìnhian ancestry into East Asia, where they interacted with the admixed descendants of ancient Fujian and local Guangxi populations. This interpretation is further supported by proposed Hòabìnhian cultural material at other southern Chinese archeological sites (although not at Baojianshan) (Ji *et al.* 2016). The genetic results of these studies in ancient Guangxi highlight both the long-term isolation preserving the deeply branching Longlin-related population and the frequent interactions between disparate populations that have occurred in southern East Asia and northern Southeast Asia. The surprising amount of admixture identified that predated agricultural-associated expansions speaks to the broad mobility and communication networks of hunter-gatherer communities in this region.

Yellow River and North Central China

The Yellow River originates in the Bayan Har 巴颜喀拉 Mountains in Qinghai Province and flows eastward through nine Chinese provinces before emptying into the Bohai Sea. The lower reaches of the river arrive through the Zhongyuan 中原 Basin in Henan and continue on through the North China Plain to Shandong on the coast. The middle reaches of the river begin in the Loess Plateau, where the river winds through a rugged terrain of gorges, canyons, and deep valleys. The upper reaches of the river are located in the far western part of the Tibetan Plateau (Figure 2). The Yellow River Basin is one of the main centers for the development of agriculture in East Asia and is considered an important region for the origin of the modern Han ethnicity (Fei 2017). Early evidence of large-scale broomcorn and foxtail millet farming is observed among Yellow River settlements during the early Holocene, such as among the Dadiwan 大地湾 culture in the Upper Yellow River (Liu & Kong 2004), the Cishan 磁山 culture (Lu *et al.* 2009), and the Lower Yellow River Houli 后李 culture sites of Yuezhuang 月庄 (Crawford *et al.* 2006) and Xiaojingshan 小荆山

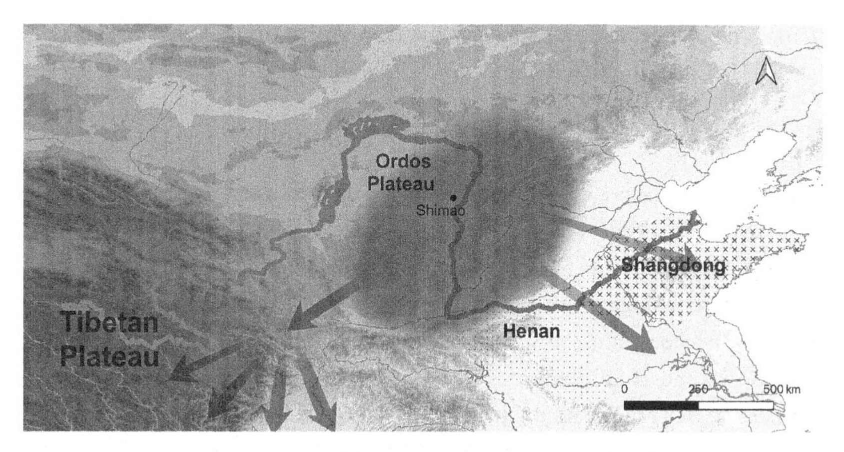

Figure 2 Featured regions along the Yellow River. A dark oval along the middle reaches represents a proposed homeland of proto-Sino-Tibetan language speakers, with suggested dispersal routes of the proto-Tibetan branch to the southwest, and proto-Sinetic branch to the east and south.

(Hu *et al.* 2008) dating to roughly 8,000 years ago. The Yellow River Basin has also been proposed as the geographical source of the Sino-Tibetan language family before its eventual dissemination to the west, east, and south likely in association with the expansion of the Yangshao 仰韶 or Majiayao 马家窑 Neolithic cultures between 4,000 and 6,000 years ago (Sagart *et al.* 2019; Zhang *et al.* 2019).

Neolithic Yellow River farmers form a genetic cluster distinct from the ANA ancestry profile to the north (Ning *et al.* 2020b; Wang *et al.* 2021a) and Fujian ancestry from the south (Wang *et al.* 2021a; Yang *et al.* 2020), and remains a dominant ancestral component of present-day northern Han Chinese (Wang *et al.* 2021a). This Yellow River ancestry can be modeled as having 90% derived from a northern inland lineage branching early from a common East Asian Tianyuan-like ancestry and 10% contribution from an equally deep branching coastal group (Wang *et al.* 2021a). The broad distribution of YR ancestry has been linked to the expansion of millet agriculturists at least since the Middle Neolithic. In addition to admixture with ANA ancestry in the agricultural Basin of the West Liao River from the Middle Neolithic described earlier, it is also found admixed with about 20% ANA ancestry at Early Bronze Age Qijia 齐家 culture sites in the Upper Yellow River, the Middle Neolithic Miaozigou 庙子沟 site in Inner Mongolia, the Late Neolithic Shimao site on the Loess Plateau (Ning *et al.* 2020b), with a similar component described in 3,400-year-old Nepalese (Liu *et al.* 2022), and it makes up approximately 50% of the ancestry at the Zongri 宗日 site in Tibet after 4,700 years ago (Wang *et al.*

2023). It also appears as a major genetic component of modern Tibetans (He *et al.* 2021; Lu *et al.* 2016; Ning *et al.* 2020b; Qi *et al.* 2013).

Lower Yellow River: Shandong

Shandong Province is a coastal region situated on the eastern North China Plain and includes the Yellow River Estuary and the Shandong Peninsula, which separates the Bohai and Yellow seas. Shandong has been home to several important archeological sites, such as the 9,500-year-old Bianbian 扁扁 Cave, and has been home to several successive Neolithic cultures. The earliest of these was the Houli culture (8,250–7,350 BP), which produced evidence of millet and rice grains, although isotopic analysis concluded that these had yet to play a significant dietary role (Hu *et al.* 2008). The Beixin 扁扁 culture (7,350–6,150 BP) practiced small-scale farming with evidence of dietary diversification, including domestic chickens (Xiang *et al.* 2014). Two major archeological cultures followed, Dawenkou 大汶口 and Shandong Longshan. The Dawenkou culture (6,000–4,600 BP), which co-existed with the larger Yangshao culture centered in the middle reaches of the Yellow River, had clear signs of social stratification, and possessed a broad agricultural suite of domestic pigs, chickens, and cattle, as well as rice and millet farming (Jin *et al.* 2016). The Songze 崧泽 and Liangzhu 良渚 cultures of the Lower Yangtze River to the South also interacted with the Dawenkou culture, and connections between the Dawenkou culture and West Liao River Basin also occurred through the Jiaodong Peninsula 胶东半岛 (Ren & Wu 2010). The Shandong Longshan culture (4,600–4,000 BP), which coincides with the Late Longshan period of Henan to the west, is known by its settlements on the plains near Mount Tai 泰山. The Shandong Longshan period saw an increased cultural and social sophistication, with the skilled production of distinctive black pottery, worked jade, and small-scale silkworm cultivation. These settlements also oversaw an agricultural shift that intensified millet production over rice, with rice appearing to be reserved primarily for human consumption, while livestock were fed millet (Weisskopf *et al.* 2015). Beginning after 4,000 years ago, historical records suggest that the Xia dynasty was established, and Chinese history entered the dynastic era (Ren & Wu 2010).

The earliest sequenced genomes from Shandong date to between 9,500 and 8,000 years ago, and have been described as having ancestry that is distinct, yet branching, from that found further inland, as represented by the contemporary 8,000-year-old Yumin 裕民 individual from Inner Mongolia, and similar to that found in the majority of present-day northern East Asians. This ancestry, known broadly as northern East Asian ancestry (nEA), likely finds its present-day wide distribution due to its association with Yellow River agricultural (YR) populations that expanded into neighboring regions during the Neolithic (Ning *et al.* 2020b; Yang *et al.* 2020) as marked by the distribution of Sino-Tibetan languages (Sagart *et al.* 2019; Wang *et al.* 2021b), but also may describe the northern East Asian ancestral substrates prior to these movements. In Early Neolithic Shandong, this ancestry is found admixed to a small degree with southern coastal ancient Fujian ancestry, in agreement with archeological evidence of communication among coastal populations increasing from the Early to Late Neolithic as expanded interactions between northern and southern coastal groups appear to have led to more homogenized populations (Yang *et al.* 2020).

Although large genomic studies of Middle Neolithic and later Shandong populations have yet to appear, maternally inherited mitochondrial ancient DNA studies have given us insights into the changing demographic structure of this region and its association with important cultural shifts. These have shown a maternal continuity in Shandong connecting the earliest Shandong individual sequenced to date, the 9,500-year-old BianBian with the populations associated with the 4,600-year-old Dawenkou culture at the Fujia 傅家 and Beiqian 北阡 sites, notably in possessing basal examples of the B5b2 haplogroup, which is still found in present-day northern East Asians. Shandong populations from this period were found having mitochondrial haplogroups that occur at high frequencies in both present-day northern (haplogroup D) and southern (haplogroups B and F) East Asians (Liu *et al.* 2021). This is consistent with the genomic data from older Shandong individuals showing a southern coastal East Asian ancestry component, and corresponds to archeological evidence linking the Beixin and Dawenkou cultures with the coastal Yangtze River Basin cultures of Maijabang and Liangzhu to the south, in particular at the Huating 华亭 site in Jiangsu (Zhang 2015). The first observation in Shandong of mitochondrial haplogroups from inland populations, such as haplogroups M8 and A, occurs 3,100 years ago, which may correspond to the expanding influence of the Longshan culture from the Middle Yellow River toward the coast, and the cultural shift to the local Shandong Longshan that began 1,500 years earlier (there are no individuals sampled from the period between 4,600 and 3,100 years ago). The connections between the beginning of the local Longshan culture and this influx of new haplogroups still need to be explored, but at some point after 4,600 years ago, we see an enriched diversity of the matrilineal structure of Shandong corresponding to a reduction of the genetic differences between coastal and inland populations. As a result of this process, present-day East Asians have a greater genetic proximity to younger rather than older Shandong populations (Liu *et al.* 2021).

Middle Yellow River: Henan

The Middle Yellow River region is located further inland from Shandong, in present-day Henan, and has had a major impact on the development of past societies in China as far back as the Neolithic period. The region's strategic location on the fertile Central Plain surrounded by rivers made it an ideal place to facilitate movement and cultural exchange, and it has long been considered the predominant center for the early beginnings of Chinese civilization (Wang & Zhao 2022; Zhang 1991). Some of the earliest evidence of agriculture has been found along the alluvial plains of the Middle Yellow River, and from the Early Neolithic a continuous sequence of influential and complex cultures emerged, including the Peiligang 裴李岗 (9,000–7,000 BP), Yangshao (7,000–5,000 BP), and Longshan cultures (5,000–4,000 BP), followed by the Bronze Age cultures of Erlitou 二里头 and Erligang 二里岗, and the Shang and Zhou dynasties.

Yellow River farmers began building semi-permanent settlements in Henan during the Yangshao period and expanded rapidly. Although Early Neolithic genomic information from Yellow River farmers is still lacking, genome-wide analysis from the Middle Neolithic Yangshao period showed the occupants of the Yangshao Wangou 汪沟 and Xiaowu 晓坞 sites had a high affinity with each other, demonstrating a genetic homogeneity among Yangshao settlements that clusters with many northern East Asian populations (Ning *et al.* 2020b). The appearance of Yangshao pottery in the western Gan-Qing region and Tibet (Han 2012), and Yangshao rammed-earth construction techniques in the Songze culture near the mouth of the Yangtze River (Kim & Park 2017), demonstrates the broad influence the Yangshao culture may have had over surrounding areas. Yangshao-associated YR ancestry from the Middle Neolithic (YR_MN) has likewise been found to be widespread among Middle Neolithic populations from the West Liao River to Inner Mongolia (Ning *et al.* 2020b) and Tibet (Wang *et al.* 2023, 2021b). Mitochondrial haplogroups distributed throughout present-day northern East Asia (e.g. haplogroups A, D4, D5, F2, and G) have been found in the majority of inhabitants of the Yangshao sites studied (Li 2015; Miao *et al.* 2021). The appearance and distribution pattern of haplogroup D5a2a1 in particular are indicative of a rapid expansion (Miao *et al.* 2021). This corresponds to the broad appearance of the Yangshao settlements over a relatively short period of time, possibly linked to the warm Mid-Holocene Climatic Optimum (Hou *et al.* 2019; Liu & Chen 2017).

During the Longshan period that followed (5,000–2,900 BP), Yellow River settlement sites are marked by an increase in the consumption of domestic animals and intensified agriculture, along with a distinctive change of pottery style, but the demographic transition between the Yangshao and Longshan cultures is not clearly understood. Longshan populations display a general genetic continuity with the previous Yangshao populations. However, compared with Yangshao populations, Longshan-associated (YR_LN) populations have a notably higher southern East Asian component, reflecting a northward gene flow from southern populations after 4,800 years ago (Li 2019; Ning *et al.* 2020b). This increasing influx of southern East Asian ancestry parallels a growth in population density and settlements during the Late Longshan period (Li *et al.* 2021). The genomic ancestries of the Middle Yellow River populations observed during the Longshan period persist into the Bronze and Iron Ages (Ning *et al.* 2020b), as do mitochondrial haplogroups D and F, having been present there since at least the Middle Neolithic (Li 2019). Compared to present-day Chinese populations, YR_MN ancestry is most similar to Naxi and Yi populations centered near the Himalayan foothills of western China, while present-day Han Chinese show additional affinities to southern coastal East Asians than Middle Neolithic or even Iron Age Yellow River populations (Ning *et al.* 2020b).

Yellow River Origins for Sino-Tibetan Languages

The Sino-Tibetan language family encompasses a large and complex assemblage of languages spoken throughout present-day China (Sinitic branch) and Myanmar, northeastern India, Malaysia, and the Tibetan Plateau (Tibeto-Burma branch). The earliest written attestations date back over 3,000 years to the Shang Dynasty in Henan (and perhaps 800 years earlier at the Middle Yellow River site of Taosi 陶寺 (Demattè 2010)). Proposals for the origin and dispersal route of this language group have included a series of outward radiations from several possible homelands: in Sichuan in southwest China (van Driem 2005), a western origin from the Tibetan Plateau or northeastern India, where the greatest linguistic diversity exists (Blench & Post 2014), and an origin among the early agricultural societies of the Middle or Upper Yellow River (Matisoff 1991). Recent linguistic and genetic studies increasingly point to an origin for the Sino-Tibetan language family to languages spoken by the Yellow River populations of the Early to Middle Neolithic. Time-calibrated Bayesian language phylogenies estimated the earliest split between Tibeto-Burman and Sinitic language groups to have occurred 7,200–8,000 years ago, with a later dispersal accompanying the introduction of millet agriculture (Sagart *et al.* 2019; Zhang *et al.* 2019). This scenario is in congruence with identification through genetics of YR ancestry universally present among speakers of Sinitic and Tibeto-Burman languages (Ning *et al.* 2020b; Wang *et al.* 2021b). Together, these results suggest a first separation of language groups at some point after 8,000 years ago, with a westward expansion of millet agriculturists speaking proto-Tibeto-Burman languages from the Middle or Upper Yellow River Basin arriving at the Tibetan Plateau at some point around 5,000 years ago, while proto-Sinetic speakers would spread east and southward across the Central Plains.

The Tibetan Plateau

The Tibetan Plateau is one of the most challenging environments ever to be inhabited by humans. With altitudes averaging higher than 4,500 meters above sea level, this hypoxic and dry environment is characterized by sparse vegetation, reduced biodiversity, and harsh, rugged terrain including arid steppes, lakes, and steep transversal valleys between soaring mountain ranges. As the highest and largest plateau on earth, it includes parts of Sichuan, Gansu, Xinjiang, and most of Tibet and Qinghai in China, as well as parts of Nepal, Bhutan, and northeastern India and Pakistan. It is also the ultimate source of the Yellow, Yangtze, Mekong, Yarlung Tsampo (Brahmaputra), and Indus rivers (Figure 3). Despite the demanding environment, it has been inhabited by modern humans for tens of thousands of years, although archeological sites predating agricultural or pastoral lifestyles are rare (Aldenderfer 2011). The Tibetan Plateau is also one of the most sparsely inhabited world regions. Over 90% of the present-day population consists of ethnic Tibetans, with the rest belonging to Han Chinese or numerous minority groups, some speaking non-Tibeto-Burman languages. Ethnic Tibetans derive the majority (74–86%) of

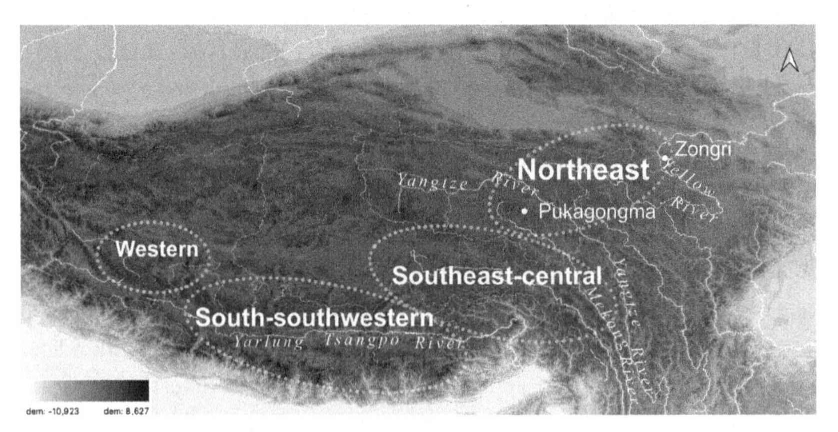

Figure 3 Geographical distribution of the four genetic clusters identified on the Tibetan Plateau. The 5,100-year-old representative population for Early Ancient Tibetan (EAT) ancestry was found at the Zongri site.

their ancestry from East Asian sources with minor components traced to South and Central Asians and Siberians (Lu *et al.* 2016; Wang *et al.* 2021a, 2023), but the origins and past distributions of these components have only recently begun to be explored through paleogenomics. Although Tibetans speak Sino-Tibetan languages associated with millet farmer expansions from the Upper and Middle Yellow River during the Neolithic, the reconstruction of their ancestries have revealed surprising complexity that does not fit a simple model of agriculturist-based expansion accompanied by local admixture.

Genetic analysis of present-day Tibetans has defined an east-west cline of ancestry shared with lowland East Asians from the eastern Tibetan slopes of Qinghai and Yunnan, which lie closest genetically to present-day Naxi, Tu, and Yi groups. The Sherpa of Nepal in the western fringe of the Tibetan Plateau occupy the furthest space along this cline, having the lowest amount of this East Asian influence, resulting in a pattern that could be explained by an isolation-by-distance model (Jeong *et al.* 2017). Supporting this model, genetic affinity between present-day plateau populations is correlated with geographic proximity, with high-altitude Tibetans clustering closely with each other, followed by lowland Amdo Tibetans from the northeastern Tibetan Plateau in China's Qinghai and Gansu Provinces, and Kham Tibetans from the southeastern regions in Sichuan and Yunnan (He *et al.* 2021).

Several non-East Asian ancestries, such as Central Asian, Siberian, and South Asian, were identified within Tibetan subpopulations as well (Lu *et al.* 2016), with Amdo Tibetans carrying 2–3% western Eurasian ancestry similar to that of Turkic-speaking Kazakh groups, and low levels of Siberian ancestry (He *et al.* 2021). Additionally, Sherpas, occupying the western plateau in present-day Nepal, have higher levels of Central Asian ancestry than that found in the central plateau (Wang *et al.* 2023), and were found to share higher genetic affinities than other Tibetans with Tibeto-Burman-speaking Nagas from north-east India, south of the Himalayas (Gnecchi-Ruscone *et al.* 2017; Liu *et al.* 2022).

East Asian Influences on Tibetan Plateau Population Structure

Several genomic analyses present evidence for an early split time between Han and Tibetan lineages predating the introduction of agriculture to the region, at either 12,600 to 6,600 (Qi *et al.* 2013), or 15,000 to 9,000 (Lu *et al.* 2016) years ago, with some uniparental markers pointing to even earlier (Qi *et al.* 2013). This raises the possibility of contacts between native Tibetans and Upper Yellow River groups prior to the Holocene, although lineage split times do not reflect actual population separation dates and do not specify where these may have occurred. Subsequent contacts or multiple migrations can also reduce these times, but additional evidence such as Sherpa and Han split times of 16,000 to 11,000 years ago and the appearance of Yellow River ancestry along the Himalayan arc far from the northeastern fringe well before the evidence of high-altitude millet farming 5,600 years ago (Lu 2023) argues for pre-agricultural interactions, perhaps at lower altitudes, with native Tibetans and Upper Yellow River foragers from Gansu, Qinghai or northern Sichuan. Such contacts would coincide with the warming climate at the close of the glacial period that may have allowed early westward migration into higher altitudes (Lu *et al.* 2016). In this scenario, agricultural-based expansions during the Majiayao period may have encountered a Tibetan substrate already admixed to some extent with northern East Asian ancestry. The early local domestication of yak dating to 7,300 years ago suggests that pastoral nomads may have preceded agricultural societies at high elevations (Qiu *et al.* 2015), who may have traded with lowland agricultural populations.

The oldest genome from the Tibetan Plateau, Zongri5.1K, dates to 5,100 years ago and was recovered from the Zongri site in the Gonghe 共和 Basin, 3,000 meters above sea level in the northeastern plateau (Wang *et al.* 2023). The Zongri culture is a local Tibetan culture with strong influence from the contemporary Maijiayao culture of the nearby Upper Yellow River region (Lancuo *et al.* 2023). Genomic information from several younger individuals dating from 4,700 to 3,900 years ago also at Zongri, as well as genomic population data from a nearby younger and higher-elevation site, the 2,900-year-old Pukagongma 普卡贡玛 site in Qinghai, offers a time transect to evaluate the Middle-to-Late Neolithic demographic patterns between the Tibetan Plateau and the Upper Yellow River populations (Figure 3). Zongri5.1K ancestry is distinct from more recent individuals from Zongri in that it lacks a southern East Asian component in addition to having reduced Yellow River ancestry, and has been used to represent Early Ancient Tibetan (EAT) ancestry. When compared with present-day individuals, EAT ancestry is highest among the Qiang, Tibetan, and Sherpa, and thus still can be found in admixed form on the Tibetan Plateau (Wang *et al.* 2023). EAT ancestry has also been identified in an individual from the 3,400-year-old site of Lubrak in the Himalayan arc (Liu *et al.* 2022). More recent Zongri individuals can be modeled as having 40–74% EAT ancestry in addition to ancestry from Early to Middle Neolithic Yellow River populations, with some additional ancestry similar to Yumin in Inner Mongolia. This influx of lowland East Asian ancestry prior to 4,700 years ago does not appear at the higher-elevation Pukagongma site nearly 2,000 years later, which could signal that Neolithic migrations into the plateau may have been sporadic and localized (Wang *et al.* 2023).

Defining the sources of East Asian ancestry found throughout the Tibetan Plateau can allow us to better understand the timing, routes, and cultural contacts underlying the Neolithic demographic shifts of the region. In general, this incoming ancestry is shared by Early and Middle Neolithic groups from the Yellow River to Inner Mongolia (Wang *et al.* 2023). In the Himalayan arc this ancestry has been shown to more closely resemble Upper Yellow River Late Neolithic populations over those belonging to the Yellow River Middle Neolithic (Liu *et al.* 2022). In addition to the majority component of Yellow River–related ancestry in Tibetans, several other sources appear at different times and places across the plateau, attesting to the multiple migrations and interactions occurring between the surrounding regions over the past few thousand years. In the eastern plateau, ancestry closely shared with an Iron Age Upper Yellow River individual from Dacaozi 大槽子 begins appearing only in the past 700 years. In the southeastern plateau, southern East Asian ancestry appears by at least 2,800 years ago, Central Asian ancestry was found dating back to 1,500 years ago, which appears to be widespread throughout the Himalayan arc, but at lower levels than in present-day Sherpa. South Asian ancestry, as represented by a Bronze Age genome from Turkmenistan, was present at levels between 6% and 14% along the western plateau in individuals dating from 2,300 years ago to recent times (Wang *et al.* 2023).

Plateau-wide population structures have also been identified. These fall into three geographic clusters of shared ancestry: a "northeast" cluster, a "southeast-central" cluster, and a "south-southwestern" cluster including the Himalayan arc in Nepal (Figure 3). Each of these showed a greater genetic diversity between them in the past than in more recent times, due to a gradual homogenization of trans-plateau populations. The south-southwestern cluster was found to closely follow the Yarlung Tsangpo River Valley, today the most populous area of the plateau, showing the importance of the river to early (before 3,400 years ago) settlement patterns and the maintenance of genetic homogeneity (Wang *et al.* 2023).

Neolithic, Late Upper Paleolithic, and Deep Paleolithic Roots

Although the admixture date of the earliest East Asian component of Tibetan genomes is estimated to the Early or pre-Neolithic (Lu *et al.* 2016; Qi *et al.* 2013), attempts to identify the divergence time of the core Tibetan founding population with the other East Asians using the coalescence times of Tibetan Y chromosome and mitochondrial haplogroups have revealed a curious pattern of Early Neolithic East Asian haplogroups mixed with much deeper branching groups either specific to Tibetans or found also in more distant populations.

Over half of Tibetans belong to the East Asian Y chromosome haplogroup D-M174, a haplogroup with origins dating 60,000 to 32,000 years ago and with sister lineages found in both the Andaman Islands and the Japanese archipelago (Liu *et al.* 2022; Qi *et al.* 2013; Shi *et al.* 2008). In contrast, the lower frequency Y haplogroup O-M117, dates up to 7,000 years ago and is common in the Upper Yellow River from the Middle to Late Neolithic where it is associated with Yangshao and Qijia agricultural cultures, respectively (Liu *et al.* 2022). Common Tibetan mitochondrial lineages also show both deeply and more recently branching haplogroups. Of the mitochondrial haplogroups found in the Tibetan Plateau, haplogroup M62 (formerly M16) dates to approximately 28,000 years ago and is rarely found outside of the region (Qi *et al.* 2013; Zhao *et al.* 2009), while M9a, found at high frequency in southern East Asians, dates to 9,500 years ago, and the Tibetan-specific haplogroup A dates from 13,000 to 7,000 years ago (Qi *et al.* 2013).

This pattern of both deep Upper Paleolithic and Early Neolithic uniparental chromosomal lineages is borne out in nuclear genomic analysis. Although the dominant ancestry across the plateau can be traced to northern East Asian sources primarily from the Yellow River Basin and Inner Mongolia dating from 9,500 to 4,000 years ago, between 6% and 26% of Tibetan genomes are derived from a deeply branching modern human ancestry of unknown origin exclusive to the Tibetan Plateau (Liu *et al.* 2022; Lu *et al.* 2016; Wang *et al.* 2023). No ancestral reference corresponding to this deeply branching "ghost" population has yet been discovered, but it has been loosely modeled as branching from an Asian lineage prior to the lineage leading to the 40,000-year-old Tianyuan, and is similarly distant from the enigmatic 45,000-year-old Siberian Ust-Ishim and the deeply branching southern East Asian branch leading to the Andaman Islanders (Önge), which has also been reported appearing at low levels along the East Asian coast, including in Paleolithic Japanese Jōmon (Wang *et al.* 2021b). There may be some link to ancient ANA ancestry as well, since statistical tests show a possible affinity to Amur River individuals from 19,000 to 14,000 years old (Wang *et al.* 2023). A competing hypothesis has proposed that this highly divergent Tibetan ancestry may have come from an extremely early modern human population from Siberia which split from other modern human lineages shortly after the Out-of-Africa event, and admixed with the remnants of admixed archaic Tibetan Plateau populations. The descendants of this population would have remained in the region until East Asians arrived on the plateau in the Early Neolithic (Lu *et al.* 2016); however, this explanation appears to be implausible since in later analyses, Tibetans appear to lack a corresponding increase in archaic ancestry (Liu *et al.* 2022; Wang *et al.* 2023). The similar proportion of this ancestry throughout the Tibetan Plateau populations signifies that it likely derives from a common source population and, thus, may represent the autochthonous Plateau population prior to the arrival of post-LGM East Asians. Given the depth of the lineages, the origin of this population may have first arrived on the Plateau prior to the LGM, and may have admixed with remnant Denisovan populations and acquired the *EPAS1* gene advantageous to high-altitude habitation (Huerta-Sánchez *et al.* 2014; Lu *et al.* 2016). This time period would be close to the most recent estimated introgression date of this allele of around 48,000 (16,000–59,500) years ago (Zhang *et al.* 2021c). A warmer humid period in the Upper Paleolithic between 40,000 and 30,000 years ago would have made the Tibetan Plateau more habitable than at the present, and may have facilitated the pre-LGM entry of early modern humans (Yang *et al.* 2004). However, selective pressure on this allele is thought not to have begun until much later (9,000 years ago) on standing variation, so the allele may have alternatively been introduced at lower altitudes (Zhang *et al.* 2021c), not rising in frequency until the receiving population later settled on the plateau. A similarity reported between Paleolithic Tibetan Plateau archeology sites and contemporary sites of East Asia may give some clues as to the geographic origin of this ghost population (Gao *et al.* 2008).

From our current understanding from ancient genetic data, the formation of the present-day Tibetan population was likely to have involved an initial migration into the Tibetan Plateau during a mild climatic period prior to the Holocene by a deeply divergent modern human 'ghost' population that has only partially been identified. No evidence of migrations into the plateau during the LGM has been found, but interactions at the eastern edge may have occurred after the climate improved. Later, increasing gene flow from surrounding lowland populations may have reached its maximum with the introduction of agriculture, followed by more sporadic migrations into historical times. Further research will be needed to more fully characterize the Upper Paleolithic substrate, as well as to elucidate the mechanisms for the formation of the observed Late Neolithic and Bronze Age population structures.

High-Altitude Adaptations: *EPAS1* and *ELGN1*

The ability of humans to live at the hypoxic high-altitudes of the Tibetan Plateau has been greatly facilitated by genetic adaptations that allow the more efficient use of oxygen by the blood in low oxygen environments. Among these, *EPAS1* and its negative regulator *ELGN1* have been identified by the strength of the selective sweeps of their diverged genetic variants (Peng *et al.* 2011). The introgressed Denisovan variant of *EPAS1* is correlated with low hemoglobin and a reduced physiological response to hypoxia. An additional beneficial

ELGN1 variant is found at frequencies of 64.3–75.8% among present-day Tibetans, with the frequency correlated to elevation. The onset of selection of the *ELGN1_D4E* allele has been estimated at 8,400 years ago. It is believed to play a role dependent upon the earlier *EPAS1* variant, improving its activity, and thus has more recent selection dynamics (Xiang *et al.* 2013). Observing the occurrence of *EPAS1* across the Plateau over the past 5,100 years revealed the oldest sample, Zongri5.1K, to have been homozygous for the derived *EPAS1* allele, and an increasing allele frequency over time could be observed (Wang *et al.* 2023). The derived *EPAS1* variant had an allele frequency among plateau populations of 36% between 5,100 and 2,500 years ago, 47% 2,400 to 1,900 years ago, and 59% 1,600 to 700 years ago (Wang *et al.* 2023), rising until the present-day frequency for the derived *EPAS1* allele among Tibetans of 86%. The rate of increase observed for the *EPAS1* allele frequency appears to support the recent selective pressure relative to the much older introgression time reported for this variant (Zhang *et al.* 2021c).

Mongolia and the Eastern Steppe

The Mongolian Plateau includes the entire area of present-day Mongolia between China and Siberia and contains a diverse geography of mountains, deserts and grasslands. It stretches from the east where the headwaters of the Amur River begin, to the Altai Mountains in the west and southwest. The Sayan Mountain range and the Khentii Mountains border its north, and the Khangai Mountains are found in its western center. These mountains feed two lake valleys, the Gobi Valley Lake region is fed by the Khangai Mountains from the north, and the Great Lakes Valley is situated in a basin between the Altai, Sayan, and Khangai Mountains in the west. The central and eastern part of the territory contains the vast Mongolian-Manchurian grassland steppe, which sits above the North China Plain. Across the southern expanse is the 1,600-kilometer-wide Gobi desert (Figure 4). Several sites attest to the presence of modern humans in Mongolia dating to the Upper Paleolithic, such as the Tolbor sites in the north (Gladyshev *et al.* 2010; Rybin *et al.* 2020; Zwyns *et al.* 2019), with archeological horizons dating from 43,000 to 15,000 years ago, or Tsagaan-Agui and Chikhen-Agui cave sites in the central Gobi (Zwyns *et al.* 2014). Overall, Holocene sites in Mongolia appear to be centered around waterways and lake basins, and the region has been assumed to have been more sparsely populated than the Lake Baikal area in Siberia to the north (Wright 2021). The 34,000-year-old skullcap from Salkhit Valley in northeastern Mongolia is the only Upper Paleolithic human material recovered thus far. The ancestry identified in the Salkhit skull, a mixture of basal East Asian

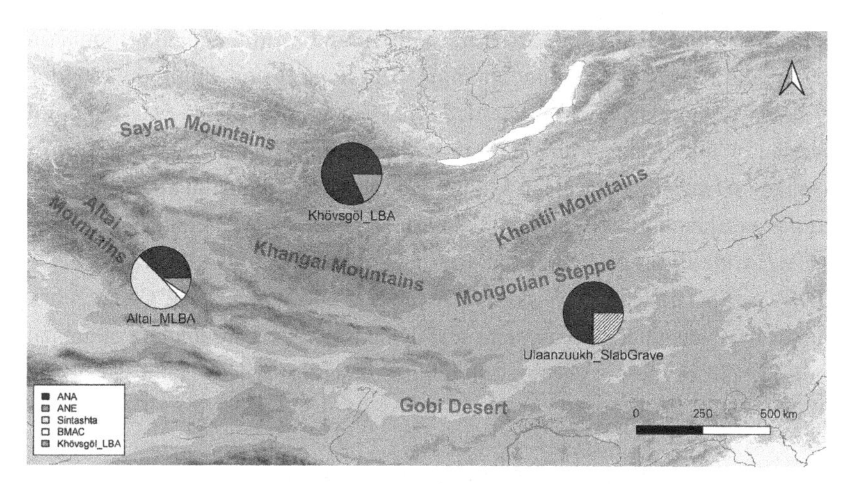

Figure 4 The genetic ancestry components and approximate distributions of the three principal populations present in Bronze Age Mongolia. Ancestry profiles adapted from Jeong *et al.* 2020 and Lee *et al.* 2023.

Tianyuan-like and ANS ancestry from Siberia, has not yet been identified in any other individual (Massilani *et al.* 2020), and had disappeared from the region prior to the mid-Holocene genomes characterized in Mongolia, most likely along with the disappearance of Tianyuan ancestry in northeastern East Asia by the LGM (Mao *et al.* 2021).

The exposed nature of much of the Mongolian landscape and the lack of large-scale, developed agriculture have made the identification of pre–Bronze Age archeological sites difficult, and much of the population history from this time period is unknown. Moreover, the nomadic practices of prehistoric populations across much of the Mongolian steppe since the Early Bronze Age restrict the detection of camps or settlements. The practice of marking burials through stones or burial mounds, beginning in the Bronze Age, has led much of the ancient genetics research to focus on the Bronze Age and following periods (Jeong *et al.* 2020). Agriculture appears to have been practiced only in a limited sense in the eastern river valleys during the Neolithic; however, the arrival of nomadic pastoralism in the Early Bronze Age had an outsized impact on the lifestyle and subsistence practices lasting for millennia (Taylor *et al.* 2019). Herding economies with domestic livestock, including sheep, goats, and cattle, appear to have been introduced more than 5,000 years ago with the arrival of the Afanasievo Cultural groups from the steppes to the west, through the Altai (Taylor *et al.* 2019). Afanasievo populations show a close affinity with the proto-Indo-European-speaking Yamnaya culture of the Pontic Steppe in eastern Europe, an affinity supported by both cultural and genetic similarities (Allentoft *et al.* 2015).

Afanasievo burials first appeared in the west and central Kanghai mountain region and feature raised stone mounds, occasionally containing the remains of domestic animals or disassembled wheeled wagons. With some temporal overlap, a similar pastoralist culture with a different mortuary tradition follows the Afanasievo burials in Mongolia (and also in the Altai and Xinjiang), known as Chemurchek. Chemurchek burials are rectangular in shape and often marked with stone stele engraved with anthropomorphic figures (Taylor *et al.* 2019). Ancient protein analysis on dental calculus of Afanasievo and Chemurchek burials have identified milk proteins that demonstrate the consumption of animal milk in both of these archeological cultures dating to at least 5,000 years ago (Wilkin *et al.* 2020).

Neolithic and Early Bronze Age

The earliest post-LGM genomes characterized in Mongolia date to the Late Neolithic and Early Bronze Age between roughly 7,000 and 5,000 years ago, and show that at this early date, the region was already home to diverse populations occupying different geographical areas. In northeastern Mongolia, Neolithic sites around the Kerulen River, associated with a hunting and fishing-based culture practicing small-scale agricultural activities, were found to have a similar ANA ancestry to that found among contemporary populations around the Amur River Basin and Primorye further east (Jeong *et al.* 2020; Wang *et al.* 2021a). In fact ANA ancestry appears to have been the primary ancestral component across much of northern and eastern Mongolia during the Late Neolithic and Early Bronze Ages. It existed unadmixed in eastern Mongolia from the Neolithic to the Middle and Late Bronze Age (MLBA), where it is also found in MLBA Ulaanzuukh culture-associated burials there. Outside of eastern Mongolia, ANA ancestry is found admixed with other minor ancestral components. A Neolithic burial near the Egiyn-Gol River Valley in northern Mongolia had ANA ancestry admixed with 17% ancestry associated with ANE-related sources. This ancestry profile matches that found at Early Neolithic Fofonovo culture burial sites further to the north surrounding Lake Baikal in Siberia, where individuals were found with ANA ancestry at 83–87% and the remainder belonging to an ANE-related component. This particular admixed ancestry persisted in the Baikal region from the Neolithic (Kitoi culture) through the Early Bronze Age (Glazkovo culture) and later, during which time the ANE component gradually rose from 6% to 20% (Barros Damgaard *et al.* 2018; Jeong *et al.* 2020).

The first appearance of western steppe cultures in Mongolia is found in the Early Bronze Age, possibly entering the region through the Upper Yenisei and

Sayan Mountains, or the Altai Mountain range (Janz *et al.* 2017). Five-thousand-year-old Afanasievo burials in Shatar Chuluu near the Khangai Mountains in central Mongolia are genetically identical to the Western Steppe Herder (WSH) ancestry found in Afanasievo groups from Yenisei in the Altai (Allentoft *et al.* 2015; Jeong *et al.* 2020; Narasimhan *et al.* 2019). This links the introduction of pastoralism in Mongolia to the eastward expansion of western steppe culture. Chemurchek burials in western Mongolia, which have been archeologically linked to sites further west (Kovalev 2016), have shown greater genetic diversity. The ancestry found at Chemurchek burials from the southern Altai site of Yagshiin Huduu could be modeled as western steppe ancestry, but with an ANE component similar to Botai groups from Kazakhstan. A smaller component was similar to ancient Iranian ancestry associated with the Central Asian Bronze Age Bactria-Margiana Archaeological Complex (BMAC), previously identified in Kazakhstan (Narasimhan *et al.* 2019). Chemurchek burials from the northern Altai, however, were characterized as 80% ANA ancestry and the rest being that of the southern Altai Chemurchek individuals, which may be explained by incoming western Chemurchek-associated groups admixing locally with ANA ancestry, perhaps in the areas around the Altai or western Sayan Mountains (Jeong *et al.* 2020). ANA ancestry also appears in Inner Mongolia to the south in the 8,400-year-old individual from Yumin village site near Wulanchabu, although at Yumin, the ANA ancestry appears admixed with East Asian ancestry along the Tibetan cline (Yang *et al.* 2020). As discussed earlier, an east-west cline among the ANA ancestry was identified, with western Mongolian sites showing an increase in ANE admixed ancestry, and in the Amur River region to the east, a component with affinity to ancestry found in Paleolithic Jōmon groups from Japan was present up to 13% (Wang *et al.* 2021a). The distribution pattern of ANA ancestry in Mongolia and surrounding regions suggests a common northern East Asian ancestry was dispersed over a wide geographical region from west Baikal in Siberia to the northeastern Asian coastal Primorye and the Amur River Basin, and south into Inner-Mongolia, admixed with ANE groups in Siberia, and occasionally with incoming Bronze Age populations from the western steppes in northwestern Mongolia. The association of this ancestry with present-day Transeurasian language speakers, as mentioned earlier, may give some indication of the geographical origins of the Transeurasian language family (Robbeets *et al.* 2021).

Three Bronze Age Populations

Large ancient genomic studies of over 300 individuals beginning with the MLBA revealed the emergence of a geographic-genetic structure across the region consisting of three distinct populations (Jeong *et al.* 2020). These ancestries have been termed Khövsgöl_LBA, Altai_MLBA, and Ulaanzuukha_SlabGrave, and are found in northern central, western, and eastern Mongolia, respectively. Khövsgöl_LBA defines the previously described ancestry with a majority ANA admixed with ANE found chiefly between the Kanghai Mountains and Lake Baikal. A genetic a continuity was found including Late Bronze Age (LBA) pastoralists and both Neolithic occupants of this region and hunter-gatherers of Lake Baikal to the north, demonstrating a persistence of this ancestry over 3,000 years in the area (Figure 4).

Altai_MLBA ancestry is defined as Khövsgöl_LBA admixed with a newly appearing western steppe ancestry matching that of Sintashta culture-associated steppe herders originating from east of the Urals (Allentoft *et al.* 2015; Narasimhan *et al.* 2019). This incoming WSH population, which had genetic links to the Corded Ware cultures of central and eastern Europe (Mathieson *et al.* 2015), likely arrived as part of an eastward expansion of Sintashta groups from the western steppe, and is found predominantly in western and northern Mongolia. Analysis of the age of admixture of this Sintashta WSH component in MLBA burials in western Mongolia estimates an arrival roughly 300 years prior to when the individuals lived, or about 3,500 years ago, and was found to be distinct from the earlier WSH ancestry associated with the Afanasievo (Jeong *et al.* 2020). This time period coincides with a rising use of horses as transport animals on the Mongolian steppe, and includes the earliest known appearance of horse milking (Wilkin *et al.* 2020). Horses associated with the Sintashta expansion are ancestral to modern domestic horses, and the intensified use of horses of this period can be linked to these incoming steppe pastoralists (Librado *et al.* 2021). Several individuals within the Altai_MLBA group required additional ancestral contributions associated with the BMAC, similar to the ancestry appearing in earlier Chemurchek individuals (Jeong *et al.* 2020). An interesting aspect of the MLBA population survey of Mongolia was the apparent replacement of much of the EBA ancestry profile found in Afanasievo and Chemurchek populations, although analysis of MLBA populations across a broader region will be required to better address the fate of these EBA populations. Altai_MLBA ancestry persisted into the Iron Age and is found along with BMAC ancestry in the succeeding Scytho-Siberian Sagly/Uyuk culture in northwestern Mongolia. This Sagly/Uyuk genetic profile, Altai_MLBA admixed with Iranian-related BMAC-like ancestry, is also represented in other Scythian-complex cultures, being similar to that of the Tagar north of the Sayan Mountains and the Saka to the west (Jeong *et al.* 2020). The evolving ancestry signatures in western Mongolia attest to the ongoing exchange and mobility between western steppe populations and inhabitants of western Mongolia since at least the Early Bronze Age.

The third ancestry identified, Ulaanzuukh_SlabGrave, was restricted to central, eastern, and southeastern Mongolia. Like contemporary groups in central and western Mongolia, the Ulaanzuukh culture also practiced a pastoralist economy, but Ulaanzuukh burials differ from those further to the west, with bodies being placed in prone position in a rectangular structure composed of flat stones, sometimes marked with undecorated standing stones (Dashtseveg *et al.* 2013). Although dating to the Late Bronze Age, Ulaanzuukh cultural material shows little use of metal, consisting primarily of stone tools and ceramics (Wright *et al.* 2019). The Ulaanzuukh_SlabGrave ancestry associated with Ulaanzuukh graves was determined to contain an average of 75% ANA, similar to the pre–Bronze Age eastern Mongolian ancestry found throughout the Amur River Basin, but with a 25% component derived from Khovsgol_LBA ancestry from northern Mongolia, with one Ulaanzuukh individual having as high as 63.5% Khovsgol_LBA. Central and eastern Mongolian individuals from the succeeding Slab Grave culture also carried this ancestry, some with even greater proportions of Khovsgol_LBA (Lee *et al.* 2023).

Xiongnu and the Formation of the Present-Day Mongolians

The genetic separation between the populations living in eastern and western Mongolia from the Neolithic to the Iron Age is remarkable, especially since the same nomadic pastoralism was practiced across the whole of Mongolia dating back to the Bronze Age, and despite the broad use of domestic animals originating from the west. This structure is indicative of a transfer of economic practices from the west to the east without a large detectable genetic impact on eastern populations. This order changes during the Xiongnu period in the Iron Age. The Xiongnu confederation, a nomadic equestrian steppe culture, is the first historically attested empire of the eastern Eurasian steppe, eventually extending from Mongolia into present-day Inner Mongolia, Russia, Kazakhstan, Kyrgyzstan, and parts of northwestern China (Miller 2024). Sixty Xiongnu burials were genetically analyzed dating from the beginning and end of the Xiongnu period, which began roughly 2,200 years ago and lasted for nearly 300 years. Although some early Xiongnu period individuals from northern central Mongolia derived the majority of their ancestry from populations similar to the Early Iron Age Scythian-complex-related Sagly/Uyuk in the Altai region of western Mongolia, admixed with approximately 8% additional Iranian BMAC ancestry, others from the same region were admixed between Sagly/Uyuk ancestry and ancestry similar to that of Ulaanzuukh_SlabGrave, still others had unadmixed Ulaanzuukh_SlabGrave ancestry (Jeong *et al.* 2020). The heterogeneity present in the early Xiongnu, which involved admixed and unadmixed Early Iron Age ancestries from across Mongolia, increased in later Xiongnu period individuals, with additional ancestral elements. In addition to more extensive admixtures involving early Xiongnu components as well as ancestries present in Mongolia during the MLBA, such as the Khövsgöl_LBA, late Xiongnu also contained ancestry related to another WSH Scythian-related culture distinct from the Sagly/Uyuk, the Sarmatians, who originated from the western Steppe of Central Asia. These results point to the continuation of interactions between western steppe cultures in Mongolia that began in the Bronze Age. An East Asian ancestry separate from ANA was also represented, close to modern-day Han Chinese, which may reflect the increasing interactions with the Han Empire, involving both military disputes and the use of marriage alliances to secure diplomatic relationships (Jeong *et al.* 2020).

After the eventual defeat of the Xiongnu by the Han dynasty, several confederations rose to power over the Mongolian Plateau. Genomic information from the medieval period Turkic and Uyghur Khagnates document a changing demography with persistently heterogeneous populations. An additional western steppe ancestry closer to the Alans than to the Sarmatians appears in several Uyghur burials, and Iranian-related and Ulaanzuukh_SlabGrave ancestry is found in both Turkic- and Uyghur-period individuals (Jeong *et al.* 2020). The Mongol Empire, which dates to the thirteenth and fourteenth centuries and eventually encompassed much of the Eurasian continent, began by uniting several diverse nomadic confederations across Mongolia and neighboring regions. Sixty-one Mongol Empire–period individuals were analyzed and exhibited a greater genetic homogeneity than the preceding populations of the region, demonstrating a close continuity with the present-day population of Mongolia. This profile is marked by an increase in East Asian genetic affinities, as well as the disappearance of ANE-related components present in earlier ancestries of the northern central and western regions. Overall, the population dating to the Mongol period consisted of three components, with the majority being represented by Ulaanzuukh_SlabGrave ancestry, and included a Han-related component and a western Eurasian component most closely matching that of the Alans (Jeong *et al.* 2020). Comparisons of Mongol-era individuals with present-day populations showed more than half of them to be closely related to present-day Mongolic language speakers. These analyses illustrate how the genetic homogenization process across the Mongolian Plateau that began with the rise of nomadic pastoralist confederations such as the Xiongnu had led to the early profile of the present-day Mongolic population by the time of the Mongol Empire.

Xinjiang

To the west of Mongolia, across the Altai Mountains, lies the Xinjiang region of northwest China. Xinjiang is composed of two large semiarid basins nearly surrounded by mountain ranges. The southern Tarim Basin is bordered by the Kunlun Mountains of the Tibetan Plateau to the south, the Pamir Mountains to the west and the Tianshan Mountains to the north, and contains the Taklamakan Desert. Although its center is too dry for permanent habitation, oases fed by rivers from the surrounding mountains supply habitable regions and farmland around the edges of the Tarim Basin. The milder Dzungarian Basin to the north sits between the Tianshan and Altai Mountain ranges, with the Tarbagatai Mountains of Kazakhstan to the northwest. Between the Tarbagatai and Altai Mountains, an area known as the Dzungarian Gate opens to the grasslands of the western steppe. On the northern side of the Tianshan Mountains, the Ili River flows northwestward into Kazakhstan. Archeological sites along the fertile plains of the Ili River Valley have documented sparse human settlements there dating back to the Paleolithic (Li *et al.* 2018), although it has been more extensively occupied since the Bronze Age (Chi & Festa 2020). Xinjiang is accessible from western Eurasia through the western steppe into the Dzungarian Basin, or through several passes over the Tianshan Mountains. From Central and South Asia the Terek Pass traverses the Pamir-Alay Mountains into the western Tarim Basin. The narrow Hexi Corridor leading to Gansu Province has been the main trade route connecting Xinjiang to the east, and Mongolia can be reached through passes through the Altai Mountains. Together, these routes constitute the Inner Asian Mountain Corridor (IAMC) by which culturally significant ideas and materials between eastern and western Eurasia were exchanged (Betts *et al.* 2019b; Frachetti 2008; Millward 2007; Spengler *et al.* 2014a) (Figure 5).

The role of Xinjiang as the gateway between east and west has placed particular importance on understanding its demographic history. It is through this region that domestic animals such as sheep, goats, and cattle and their products arrived in East Asia more than 4,000 years ago, possibly through the Hexi Corridor (Cai *et al.* 2020; Doumani Dupuy *et al.* 2023). Agricultural crops such as East Asian millets first appear in the west at a similar time in present-day Kazakhstan (Miller *et al.* 2016; Spengler *et al.* 2014b), and western crops such as wheat and barley make their first appearance in East Asia in Xinjiang and the Altai region in association with Bronze Age pastoralists (Lu *et al.* 2019; Zhou *et al.* 2020). Further evidence of western cultural presence in Xinjiang can be found in the discovery of third- to eighth-century CE texts written in an early-branching Indo-European language family known as Tocharian (Peyrot 2017). The proto-Tocharian lineage has been estimated to have split from the western branches of Indo-European about 5,000 years ago, and have been associated with the Afanasievo culture (Anthony & Ringe 2015; Kassian *et al.* 2021). Indo-Iranian languages were also spoken in Xinjiang with the arrival of the Saka and

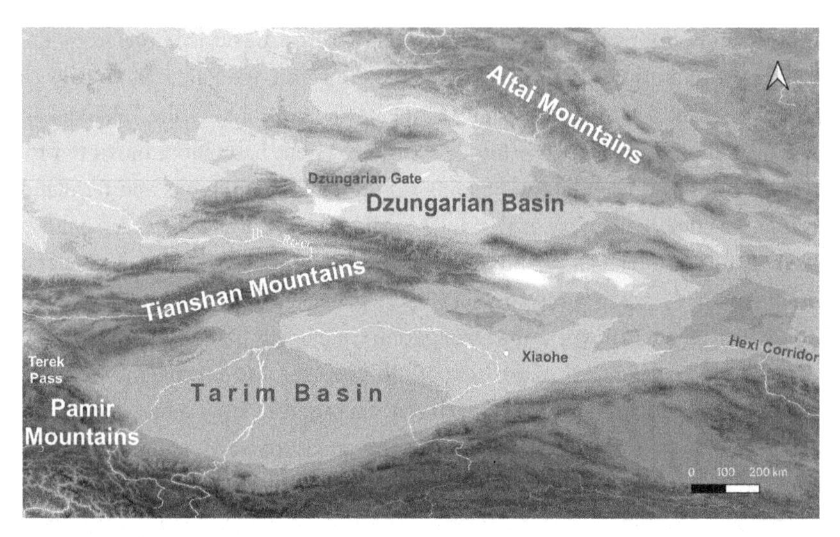

Figure 5 Geography of Xinjiang and surrounding regions. Relevant features highlighted include the Terek Pass leading to Central and South Asia, the Hexi Corridor to East Asia, and the Dzungarian Gate accessing the Kazakh Steppe.

in the Iron Age Kingdom of Khotan, which extended across the western Tarim Basin (Bailey 1970).

The origins of the earliest inhabitants in Xinjiang have been the subject of intense focus by archeologists and paleoanthropologists for decades, with special attention regarding the oldest Bronze Age burials in the Tarim Basin: the Tarim mummies. Two competing hypotheses, both proposing a dual-layered origin, have been offered to explain the origin of Tarim Basin populations, with the primary layer composed of either Bronze Age steppe pastoralists, such as the Afanasievo- or Chemurchek-related groups, or a the BMAC agriculturalists centered around the Amu Darya River in Central Asia across the Pamir Mountains. A secondary influence from Andronovo-related MLBA pastoralists is featured in both. The steppe origin finds support in physical anthropological data, cultural artifacts, and mortuary practices, and may also provide a link with the arrival of Tocharian (Han 1999; Kuzmina 1998; Mallory & Mair 2000), whereas similarities in agricultural practices and textiles, as well as the ritual use of ephedra support a BMAC-related origin (Betts *et al.* 2019a; Hemphill & Mallory 2004; Xie *et al.* 2013). Recent paleogenomics research has been able to bring some clarity to the evidence.

The Tarim Basin Mummies

Numerous burial sites around the Tarim Basin have been excavated containing the naturally mummified remains of Bronze and Iron Age individuals. These sites date from 4,100 to 2,000 years ago, placing the older burials among the earliest Holocene archeological cultures in the region. Both western and eastern Eurasian physical characteristics have been reported among these mummies, and the grave goods associated with them, such as fermented cheese, as well as their woolen clothing, suggest a western Eurasian steppe origin (Abuduresule *et al.* 2007; Mallory & Mair 2000; Thornton & Schurr 2004; Yang *et al.* 2014b). Domestic grains of both western wheat and eastern millet have also been recovered from some of the graves (Yang *et al.* 2014a). Given the western Eurasian features of these burials, it has been proposed that these populations may have been descended from Indo-European groups who brought Tocharian languages into the region (Hemphill & Mallory 2004; Peyrot 2017). Among the oldest of these was found near Xiaohe 小河 in the eastern Lop Nur region of the Tarim Basin. Mitochondrial and Y-chromosome analyses of this site had identified a mixture of western Eurasian haplogroup lineages, such as H, U5, and K, as well as eastern haplogroups such as D and C4, similar to those found in southern Siberia, demonstrating that both western and eastern Eurasians inhabited the Tarim Basin in the Bronze Age. Individuals from more recent layers also carried haplogroups more commonly found in South and Central Asia, such as U7 and M5, which may perhaps represent a later arrival of BMAC-related ancestry. The Y-chromosome haplogroup R1a1a, associated with the MLBA Andronovo western steppe culture, was found among several males (Li *et al.* 2010, 2015). Together, these results were the first genetic confirmations of eastern and western origins of the Tarim Basin mummies.

Genomic analysis of Xiaohe, Gumugou 古墓沟 burial sites in the eastern, and Beifang 克里雅河北方 in the southern Tarim Basin gave a fuller picture of the ancestral origins of the Tarim Basin mummies, and how these populations have changed over time. In contrast to the earlier mitochondrial and Y-chromosome findings, individuals from the oldest layers of the eastern sites were found to lack any western steppe ancestry, but instead showed 72% of their ancestry being enriched in an ANE component that closely matched the 16,000-year-old Mesolithic individual Afontova Gora 3 from the Yenisei River in Siberia, and the remainder being similar to Early Bronze Age ancestry from the Baikal region. This ancestral profile, known as Tarim_EMBA1 ancestry, is believed to have represented the ancestry present in the region prior to the arrival of groups from the west. The Beifang site further to the south had a similar ancestry profile, but with slightly more Baikal_EBA ancestry. The identification of Tarim_EMBA1 ancestry allowed Baikal_EBA ancestry to be alternatively described as a mixture of 75% ANA ancestry and 25% Tarim_EMBA1. Furthermore, the Tarim ancestries were relatively homogeneous with low levels of diversity, pointing to a possible population bottleneck, and were found to have been genetically isolated for an extended period, with the estimated date of the admixture of the ANA and Baikal_EBA ancestries to have been roughly 9,000 years ago (Zhang *et al.* 2021b). Proteomic analysis of the dental calculus of several mummies confirmed the adoption of dairy consummation in this population; even though similar to other pastoralists of Mongolia, they lacked the allelic variants conferring lactase persistence (Zhang *et al.* 2021b). This also indicates an early adoption of pastoralism, and other western influences, in the Tarim Basin independent of genetic exchange. While the language spoken by the EMBA Tarim Basin populations is unknown, these results cast doubt that Tocharian was spoken among them at this time, at least prior to interactions with Afanasievo-related groups.

Bronze Age Xinjiang

The timing and means by which western Eurasian and other ancestries arrived to the Tarim Basin populations were addressed by larger ancient genomic studies of Bronze Age populations across the broader Xinjiang region. Genomic analysis of twenty individuals from six sites in northern, western, and southern Xinjiang identified four ancestries that were already admixed to various degrees during the Bronze Age in the northern and northwestern regions. In the Ili River Valley and northern Xinjiang near the Altai Mountains, the dominant Bronze Age ancestries were ANE (similar to Tarim_EMBA1), and Afanasievo-related ancestry, with a minor East Asian ANA ancestry modeled by Neolithic Baikal populations, and a rare Central Asian BMAC-related component (Kumar *et al.* 2022). Most of the individuals had a high affinity for each other, showing some degree of local homogeneity, but overall ancestry components were highly dynamic between populations and individuals, with several outliers being relatively unadmixed. Afanasievo-related ancestry demonstrates the establishment of Indo-European western steppe herders in Xinjiang, and was further supported by the appearance of Afansievo-associated Y-haplogroup R1b1a in 67% of the individuals with Afanasievo ancestry. One 5,000-year-old individual of the Songshugou site in the north was found to contain 92% East Asian-related ancestry, more similar to that found at the contemporary Shamanka site in the Baikal region than to Mongolian ANA sources, with the rest of this ancestry being Tarim_EMBA1. Two Chemurchek-associated individuals contained a BMAC component, and showed a similar genetic profile to Chemurchek populations from Mongolia discussed previously, confirming a trans-Altai genetic continuity among Chemurchek culture. The date of the integration of this BMAC component was estimated to have occurred between 5,300 and 4,600 years ago, more recent than the admixture date of ANA ancestry in

Xinjiang populations, which was approximately 6,400 years ago. The BMAC component overlaps slightly with the admixture date calculated for admixture with Afanasievo-related ancestry of between 4,900 and 4,600 years ago. Together, these dates can give a broad idea of the relative sequence of the interactions of different ancestries in the region. Although a larger population sampling would be needed to better refine these estimated dates of admixture, the Afanasievo admixture date does support the linguistic evidence of the timing of the splitting of Tocharian languages from the rest of the Indo-European family (Kumar *et al.* 2022). Another study centered around the Dzungarian Basin of five individuals from three 5,000-year-old sites associated with the Afanasievo culture showed similar genetic profiles, having ancestral components of 50–70% Afanasievo-related, 19–36% Tarim_EMBA1 (ANE), and 9–21% Baikal_EBA (ANA). This study found that this profile, Dzungharian_EBA, could further be used to model Chemurchek-associated ancestry as a mixture of Dzungarian_EBA, Tarim_EMBA1, and BMAC, giving a clearer picture of the formation of Chemurchek populations (Zhang *et al.* 2021b).

Archeological evidence records the appearance of Andronovo and Sintashta cultures in the Tianshan Mountains by the beginning of the MLBA at least 3,000 years ago (Betts *et al.* 2019b), sometimes referred to as the Eastern Fedorovo variant (Jia *et al.* 2017). Although genetically similar, individuals associated with the Andronovo and the preceding Sintashta WSH cultures can be differentiated from earlier Afanasievo-related WSH individuals by the presence of Anatolian farmer ancestry, which is assumed to have been derived from interactions with European agriculturalists of the Corded Ware culture (Allentoft *et al.* 2015; Damgaard *et al.* 2018). The transition to the MLBA in north and northwest Xinjiang is indeed marked by an increase of Anatolian farmer ancestry, with one individual from the Ili Valley having unadmixed Sintashta ancestry (Kumar *et al.* 2022). A separate genomic study of an individual from the Baigetuobie 拜格托别 site of the eastern Tianshan Mountains documents an Andronovo-associated ancestry in Xinjiang as early as 3,600 years ago (Zhu *et al.* 2021). Combined with the archeological data, these results together confirm that from the onset, the MLBA expansion of Andronovo steppe cultures into Xinjiang involved the migration of populations associated with these cultures rather than the horizontal spreading of Andronovo cultural material.

The question of the origin of the earliest Holocene Xinjiang populations thus becomes more complex than the prevailing hypotheses. We note the presence of groups bearing ancestry from the steppes, Central and South Asia, as well as East Asian ancestry from Siberia are all established in Xinjiang at the beginning of the Bronze Age. While the sources of the BMAC component can be explained through contact with the Chermurchek-related populations in the Altai region, arrival of this ancestry into Xinjiang through the IAMC route cannot be discounted. Surprisingly, the earliest human remains from the Tarim Basin were found to belong to neither of these groups, but to represent a deeply branching, seemingly earlier substrate of the most recently surviving carriers of ANE ancestry from Paleolithic Siberia, the unadmixed form of which has vanished from present-day populations (Raghavan *et al.* 2014). These people appeared to have practiced an agro-pastoralist culture that adopted material and domestic animals from the western steppe and Central Asian traditions, which, along with their associated ancestries, have been active in northern Xinjiang at least 1,000 years earlier, before eventual genetic exchange reached Xiaohe. Around the Dzungarian Basin, the Tarim_EMBA1 ancestral component found admixed with WSH and ANA groups indicates that perhaps they once occupied a larger territory, but more genetic information from earlier, pre–Bronze Age populations will need to be recovered before the population history of the Bronze Age people of the Dzungarian Basin can be more fully reconstructed.

Iron Age and Present-Day Populations

As in Mongolia, the onset of the Iron Age saw an increase in mobility linked to nomadic equestrian expansions, which is marked by a new influx of ancestry from surrounding regions into Xinjiang. Along with the continued increase in Andronovo-associated steppe MLBA ancestry, an increase in both BMAC ancestry from Central Asia and diverse East Asian ancestries is observed. Despite the growing spread of MLBA steppe ancestry, distinct Afanasievo-related EBA steppe ancestry still remained in the region. An analysis of the Iron Age site of Shirenzigou 石人子沟 in the Dzungarian Basin found the inhabitants to be composed of Saka and Afanasievo steppe ancestry without any evidence of Anatolian farmer components that would indicate Andronovo gene flow (Ning *et al.* 2019). In other sites, these two WSH ancestries were found to co-exist, with both Afanasievo-associated R1b and Andronovo-associated R1a1a Y-chromosome haplogroups being observed during this period. Populations at four sites were found to be admixed between the two steppe ancestries, presenting examples of preexisting Afanasievo-related descendants integrating with, rather than being replaced by, more recently arriving Andronovo populations (Kumar *et al.* 2022).

The increasing BMAC ancestry in the Iron Age has been linked to incoming migrations of the Saka, an Indo-Iranian-speaking tribe of the broader Scythian Cultural group who appeared in the eastern Kazakh Steppe and Tianshan mountains in the first millennium BCE, before later settling in the Tarim Basin (Kuz'mina & Mallory 2007). In the Tarim Basin, the Saka confederacy controlled a large region centered on the city of Khotan until their defeat by the Turkic Kara-Khanid Khanate in 1006 CE (Millward 2007). Saka ancestry from Tianshan has been modeled broadly as a largely MLBA steppe ancestry admixed with East Asian ancestry from southern Siberia, and Iranian ancestry related to the BMAC component (Damgaard *et al.* 2018; Jeong *et al.* 2020), which may have increased throughout the Iron Age (Gnecchi-Ruscone *et al.* 2021). In some individuals, a new South Asian component related to Andaman Islanders (Önge) also appears, possibly reflecting changing population dynamics and expanded contacts between Central and South Asia through the IAMC (Kumar *et al.* 2022).

Not only was the increase in East Asian ancestry signifying greater contacts between Xinjiang and East Asia, but the sources of East Asian ancestry are also seen to expand. The ANA-associated ancestry from southern Siberia and Mongolia that was present during the Bronze Age continued to increase, which may in part have been due to the diffusion of the Scythian-related Pazyryk culture of the Altai region (Kumar *et al.* 2022). Additionally, ancestry more closely related to the Xiongnu, as well as YR and present-day Han ancestry, began to appear. These newer ancestries mirror the westward expansion of the Xiongnu as they attempted to establish control of the region (Millward 2007). Expanding trade networks and military contacts with the Qin and Han Dynasties through the Hexi corridor are also a likely source for incoming YR-related ancestries (Allen *et al.* 2022). New East Asian Y-chromosome haplogroups such as O3a2c make their first appearance in southern and eastern Xinjiang during the Iron Age (Kumar *et al.* 2022). Population profiles of the following historical period of Xinjiang closely resembled those of the preceding Iron Age, clustering mostly with the Saka and Steppe populations, but also representing individuals with elevated East Asian or BMAC-related ancestry. Population continuity with these groups can still be detected among some Xinjiang populations. Iron Age Xinjiang ancestral components are found in present-day Uyghur and Central Asian genomes, with increased steppe ancestry in Iron Age individuals corresponding to increased affinity to present-day Uyghur populations (Kumar *et al.* 2022). The intricacy of population and cultural interactions as shown through paleogenomic analysis of Xinjiang, arguably the most demographically complex East Asian region yet studied, has given valuable insights to previous ideas of population migrations and the communication networks through which both cultural material and ideas flowed as they transfer between the eastern and western divisions of the continent. There are still mysteries, however, regarding the role this region may have played prior to the Bronze Age, although the paucity of human remains from this time period promise further research in this area to be challenging.

The Japanese Archipelago

The oldest archeological evidence of human activities on the Japanese islands dates to the Paleolithic, 38,000 years ago, and the oldest human remains include the Minatogawa 港川 and Yamashita 山下 specimens found on Okinawa island and the Pinza-Abu remains on Miyako Island, which date to between 20,000 to 32,000 years ago (Nakagawa *et al.* 2010; Suzuki & Hanihara 1982). At points throughout the Pleistocene, various islands of the Japanese archipelago were connected with each other and the mainland at several places. The most recent mainland connection emerged around 60,000 years ago from the shallower straits to the north and connected Hokkaido to the continental Primorye and Amur regions via Sakhalin Island (Ono 1990), until the Soya Strait was submerged by rising sea levels, possibly as late as 12,000 years ago (Ohshima 1990). Watercraft had been recorded during the Japanese Paleolithic (Habu 2010), which may have allowed access to the Japanese islands from the south by overseas routes at this time.

The earliest cultural period of the Japanese archipelago, the Jōmon culture appears at some point before 16,000 years ago, and is linked to one of the earliest pottery traditions in the world (Nakamura *et al.* 2001). The Jōmon period extended over 13,000 years and evolved from a hunter-gatherer and fisher subsistence mode into adopting a strategy incorporating some degree of local agriculture (Crawford 2011). They developed an increasingly sedentary lifestyle, constructed pit dwellings (Pearson 2006), and were assumed to have practiced open-sea fishing, as fishing material and dugout canoes have been excavated from Jōmon sites (Habu 2010). The Jōmon period lasted until the transition to the Yayoi culture and the Japanese Neolithic, which began 3,000 to 2,300 years ago, and is associated with the arrival of Mumun culture-associated migrants from the Korean Peninsula (Boer *et al.* 2020). The Yayoi 弥生 Period oversaw the wide-scale introduction of wet-rice and cereal farming from the coastal mainland, as well as changes in social structure and architectural and pottery styles (Crawford 2011; Miyamoto 2019). It is believed that the Yayoi period also marked the introduction of Transeurasian languages to the archipelago (Robbeets *et al.* 2021). The next important cultural transition, the Kofun 古坟 Period, began 1,700 years ago, and was characterized by an increased cultural, economic, and social influence from China and the Korean Peninsula, which included the introduction of Buddhism and the Chinese writing system.

Political centralization and the emergence of powerful clans also began during this time, and the Japanese Imperial House was established at the end of the Kofun Period in 539 CE (Mizoguchi 2002).

Jōmon Origins

The origin of the Paleolithic population of the Japanese islands has been of high interest due, on one hand, to the evidence of extended cultural continuity throughout this period (Habu 2004), and on the other, to the stark morphological differences observed between Paleolithic remains and contemporary mainland East Asians and Japanese. A degree of morphological diversity has also been identified among Jōmon populations, and skeletal and dental features of different populations were found to resemble either Southeast Asians (Matsumura *et al.* 2019; Turner 1987), Upper Paleolithic Asians (Yamaguchi 1982), or Northeastern Asians (Hanihara & Ishida 2009), as well as present-day indigenous populations of the Ainu of Hokkaido and Ryukyu Islanders (Jinam *et al.* 2015; Yamaguchi 1982). In contrast to this, the similarity of many present-day Japanese with mainland East Asians has led to the proposal of a dual-layer model of Japanese population origins. In this model, a morphologically distinct founding population, represented by the Paleolithic Jōmon, which may be ancestral to Ainu and Ryukyu Islanders, is later admixed with groups arriving from the Korean Peninsula during the Neolithic (Hanihara 1991). Early attempts to identify the genetic origin of the Jōmon people used mitochondrial, Y-chromosome, and low-coverage genomic information. These studies confirmed the uniqueness of Jōmon populations, and proposed various influences from Tibetans, Southern Siberians (Adachi *et al.* 2011; Kanzawa-Kiriyama *et al.* 2013), or Andaman Island-related Hòabìnhian from Southeast Asia (McColl *et al.* 2018). A Tibetan link was argued based on the presence of the deeply branching Y-chromosome haplogroup D-M55, which is present in a majority of Ainu (Hammer *et al.* 2006; Watanabe *et al.* 2019) and is a sub-branch of the rare D-M174 found at high frequency in Tibet (Qi *et al.* 2013; Shi *et al.* 2008). Proposed gene flow from southern Siberia relied on mitochondrial haplogroups predominant among Hokkaido and Honshu Jōmon-associated individuals and also found among southern Siberians, but rare in present-day Japanese and other East Asian groups, such as N9b, a lineage dating to 22,000–20,000 years ago (Adachi *et al.* 2011; Jinam *et al.* 2015; Kanzawa-Kiriyama *et al.* 2013). Some clarity was brought to these early findings by more recent studies involving higher coverage ancient genomic DNA from additional ancient Jōmon individuals. Despite the shared rare Y-chromosome haplogroup connection, no special genomic affinities were detected between Jōmon and either ancient or modern Tibetans (Boer *et al.* 2020; Gakuhari *et al.* 2020; Kanzawa-Kiriyama *et al.* 2019). Nor was any specific gene flow from Hòabìnhian found (Boer *et al.* 2020; Cooke *et al.* 2021; Gakuhari *et al.* 2020; Yang *et al.* 2020), although it should be noted that one group was able to model Jōmon as containing 44% of a component related to Andaman Islanders (Önge), which is also found in Hòabìnhian. Since traces of this deeply branching ancestry have been found along coastal Southeast Asian populations, this was proposed to be a remnant of an initial coastal migration route populating East Asia (Wang *et al.* 2021b). These higher-resolution analyses did identify elements of shared genetic ancestry between Jōmon and coastal, but not inland, populations from both northern and southern East Asia, especially from eastern Siberia, such as Okhotsk-Primorye region populations of coastal Siberia and the Ami and Ayatal Austronesians from the island of Taiwan, as well as coastal southern East Asians (Boer *et al.* 2020; Gakuhari *et al.* 2020; Kanzawa-Kiriyama *et al.* 2019; Wang *et al.* 2021b; Yang *et al.* 2020). Whether this signal represents a deep ancestral current indicative of an early coastal route into East Asia or more recent interactions among coastal populations, or perhaps both, has yet to be fully investigated. An additional mystery comes from studies reporting some degree of gene flow between Jōmon and ANS ancestry represented by the Upper Paleolithic Yana of northern Siberia (Cooke *et al.* 2021; Osada & Kawai 2021). One explanation may be that Tianyuan-like early ancestors of the Jōmon interacted with groups that entered Siberia through a northern migration route (Osada & Kawai 2021), but this possible connection will require a richer dataset than currently exists to better understand.

The current understanding is that the Jōmon represent a distinct East Asian lineage that separated from the basal East Asian lineage between 38,000 and 25,000 years ago, after the divergence of Tianyuan-related and Önge-related lineages, but prior to the separation of northern and eastern Asians and groups that would contribute to Native Americans (Kanzawa-Kiriyama *et al.* 2019) (Figure 1). They appear to have remained in relative isolation, although possibly periodically interacting with neighboring mainland coastal groups. Runs of Homozygosity analysis estimates that the Jōmon were likely to have gone through a population bottleneck and have maintained a relatively small population size. Another analysis proposes a more recent population split time of between 20,000 and 15,000 years, which may have been related to the closing of the last land route to the islands (Cooke *et al.* 2021; Kanzawa-Kiriyama *et al.* 2019), and is more in line with coalescence estimates for the deeply branching mitochondrial and Y-chromosome haplogroups found at high frequency in Jōmon populations, N1b and D-M55, respectively (Kanzawa-Kiriyama *et al.* 2019).

The Jōmon contribution to indigenous ethnic populations of the Japanese islands, the Ainu of the northern islands and the Ryukyuans of the Ryukyu island chain to the south, has also been examined using both modern and ancient genetics. Anthropologists have long proposed a common origin connecting the two aboriginal groups inhabiting the extreme ends of the Japanese islands (Baelz 1911), which has underlain the development of the dual-layer model. This was demonstrated by genomic analysis of modern populations that found Ainu and Ryukyuans clustering tightly together, followed by the present-day Japanese population (Japanese Archipelago Human Population Genetics Consortium 2012). Although both of these groups showed more recent admixture from mainland sources, gene flow from Austronesian sources was minimal in Ryukyuans, despite an Austronesian cultural influence observed in the southern Ryukyu islands dating to the Neolithic (Sato *et al.* 2014). The availability of the first ancient Jōmon genome established the genetic continuity of the Jōmon with the Ainu and Ryukyuans (Kanzawa-Kiriyama *et al.* 2017), with the Ainu exhibiting additional admixture from eastern, but not central Siberia (Adachi *et al.* 2018; Jeong *et al.* 2016). The common Jōmon source connecting geographically dispersed present-day indigenous groups provides genomic support to the dual-layer model. Whether the most ancient remains found in the Japanese archipelago also belong to Jōmon populations has not yet been convincingly determined. The oldest Jōmon genomic data presently dates to 9,000 years ago (Cooke *et al.* 2021), and earlier human remains have yet to be analyzed genomically. The mitochondrial haplogroup of the 20,000-year-old Minatogawa individual from Okinawa belonged to an extinct lineage of haplogroup M, which occupied a phylogenetic position basal to both Jōmon and mainland East Asian mitochondrial genomes, confounding a precise ancestral assignment (Mizuno *et al.* 2021). Successful recovery of genomic data from Upper Paleolithic sites found throughout the Japanese islands will bring more clarity to early Jōmon origins and the peopling of the archipelago.

Three-Source Origin of the Modern Japanese Population

Ancient genomes from the Jōmon, Yayoi, and Kofun periods have allowed a more thorough testing of the dual-model explanation of the population structure of present-day Japan, and have resulted in the recent inclusion of an additional third layer. Genomes from the Yayoi Period attest that the expansion of large-scale agricultural practices introducing wet-rice and cereal cultivation across Japan was accompanied by a substantial amount of admixture with Northern East Asian ancestry from the mainland. This mainland ancestry was found not to derive from the YR-related farmer dispersal from the Yellow River

Valley, but instead to share the most alleles with West Liao River millet farmers from the Middle Neolithic to the Bronze Age. High affinities with ancient Baikal and eastern Siberian populations could be explained by the large component of ANA ancestry in these populations, and West Liao River farmers with greater YR content shared fewer alleles with Yayoi (Cooke *et al.* 2021). This narrows the window of possible migration times from the West Liao River region, since YR ancestry increased in the West Liao region during the Neolithic, before decreasing in the Bronze Age (Ning *et al.* 2020b). The incoming agriculturalists were likely descendants of Middle Neolithic West Liao River populations containing a low YR ancestry component. The source and timing of this migration also support the agricultural-linked expansions associated with the spreading of Transeurasian languages, and it is thus likely that the Yayoi Period introduced proto-Japonic languages to the Japanese islands by 2,300 years ago (Robbeets *et al.* 2021). Although rice was not cultivated in the West Liao River, the population migrating into Japan from the southern Korean Peninsula was assumed to have belonged to the Mumun culture 无纹陶器时代, whose origins, based on shared features of ceramic styles, were linked to the Pianpu 偏堡 culture from the Liangdong region south of the Liao River (Miyamoto 2022) (Figure 6). Rice farming had previously spread from Shandong to the Liangdong Peninsula after 4,500 years ago (Whitman 2011), where wet-rice farming was widely adopted by the Middle Mumun Period (Crawford & Lee 2003). Two Yayoi-associated genomes were found to have contained roughly similar admixed amounts of Middle Neolithic West Liao River and Jōmon ancestry, although it should be noted the skeletons of the individuals analyzed showed greater morphological similarities with Jōmon than typical Yayoi-associated remains (Cooke *et al.* 2021). Given the present-day persistence of Jōmon-related Y-chromosome and mitochondrial haplogroups in Japan, the Yayoi Period contacts between the two populations may have been more equitable than is seen with other insular agricultural expansions, for example, in Britain, where preexisting hunter-gatherer Y-chromosome haplogroups were largely replaced (Brace *et al.* 2019).

Kofun Period genomes include the ancestry present during the preceding Yayoi Period, but add to this an additional component of mainland East Asian ancestry, best modeled as Han Chinese. This newer component, which accounts for approximately 60% of Kofun genomes, likely represents new migrations accompanying the expanding economic and political coordination between China, Korea, and Japan during the Kofun Period (Cooke *et al.* 2021). The Kofun burials studied belonged to individuals from the same site, and were not associated with the keyhole-shaped elite tombs the period was known for.

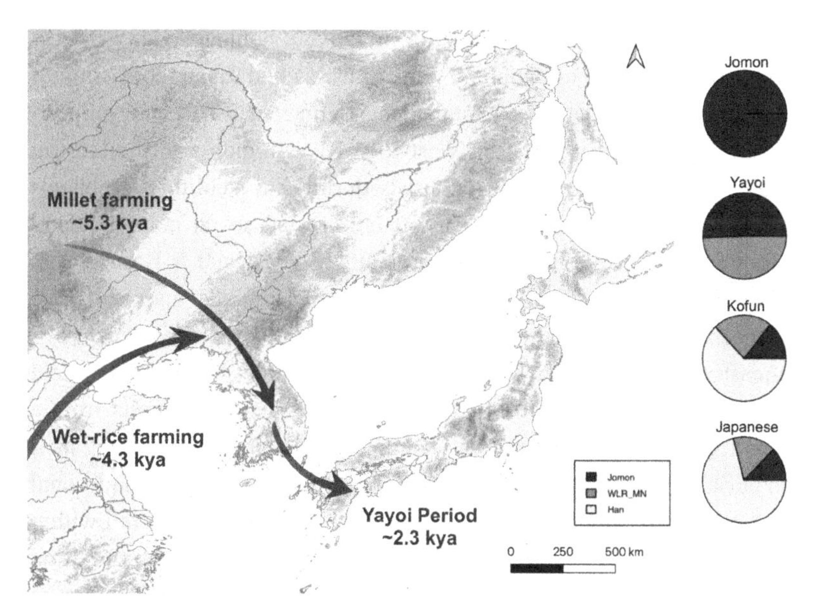

Figure 6 The origins of modern Japanese. Middle Neolithic movements of farmers from the West Liao River region (WLR_MN) may have brought wet-rice farming practices originating from Shandong first to the Korean Peninsula and later, during the Yayoi period, to the Japanese Archipelago. Han ancestry migrated from the mainland to Japan during the Kofun Period (~1.7 kya). Kya = kiloyears ago.

Additional Kofun genomes may better explain the status and role these newer East Asian immigrants played in the Kofun society. The genomic profile describing the Kofun-era individuals largely reflects the current genomic profile of Mainland Japan, as present-day Mainland Japanese have been modeled as having an average of 70% Han-related and 10% Jōmon-related ancestry, with the rest being derived from northeast East Asians (Cooke *et al.* 2021).

The Korean Peninsula

The genetic history of the Korean Peninsula is still in the early stages of being written, and few ancient genomic studies there have been completed. The oldest modern human site contains several individuals dated up to 40,000 years old from Ryonggok Cave 龙谷洞 in the mountainous area east of Pyongyang. In all, fewer than ten Pleistocene cave sites have been reported that contain either archaic or modern humans (Bae & Guyomarc'h 2015), and genetic analysis has yet to be undertaken on the majority of material recovered. Analysis of contemporary Korean genomes compared to ancient

East Asian genomic reference data shows relatively homogeneous genomic profiles, similar to those of people in parts of China and Japan, consisting of northern and southern East Asian components (Kim *et al.* 2020), and supporting the entry of ancestry from the West Liao River region into the Korean Peninsula by rice and cereal agriculturists during the Neolithic (Robbeets *et al.* 2021; Wang *et al.* 2021b). The picture created so far comes mostly from four Neolithic individuals on the southern coast and a Bronze Age individual from the eastern coast having either unadmixed mainland East Asian ancestry similar, but not exclusive, to West Liao River ancestry, or this ancestry admixed with Jōmon ancestry, with the Jōmon component ranging from 13% to 95% (Robbeets *et al.* 2021). Genomic results from a 1,700- to 1,500-year-old elite funerary complex and nearby lower-status shell mound burials in Daesung-dong 台城洞, South Korea, reveal some additional information of past population profiles. The dates of these burials fall within the Three Kingdoms Period, a time of cultural and political unification lasting from the third to the seventh centuries BCE. The eight individuals could be grouped into two distinct ancestry profiles, six as TK_1 and two as TK_2. All of them had elements of Jōmon ancestry, with the TK_1 containing 7% Jōmon and TK_2 having an elevated Jōmon component of 33%, with the remainder of both belonging to northeastern East Asian ancestry. It was also found that several Korean individuals from the Middle Neolithic could act as single sources for some TK_2 individuals, and half of the TK_1 individuals could be modeled as single sources for present-day Koreans, displaying a lengthy genetic continuity on the Korean Peninsula. Phenotypic testing of the burials found a high instance of Myopia susceptibility, which is still found in some present-day Korean populations (Wang & Wang 2022).

These analyses revealed a past Korean population more heterogeneous than that of the present-day, and demonstrated that the high levels of Jōmon ancestry identified in the Neolithic Korean Peninsula were present well into the historic period. Another analysis using diverse modern genomes from present-day Koreans combined with ancient Jōmon data identified an average of 5% Jōmon ancestry is still present among Korean people (Adachi *et al.* 2021). Later or continuing migrations from northeastern Chinese sources could account for the dilution of the Jōmon fraction. The source of the Jōmon ancestry present on the Korean Peninsula has not been identified, and it remains to be seen whether it represents migrations from the Japanese Islands or an indigenous ancestry that may have occupied the region prior to the Neolithic. If it did arrive from the Japanese Islands, whether it dates to Yayoi Period interactions, appeared before, or involved multiple events is also not clear.

Conclusions

The newfound awareness displayed in the preceding sections, of both the initial peopling of East Asia and the subsequent population movements over the ensuing millennia, is a stark witness of the strength of ancient DNA studies to uncover aspects of prehistory that were previously unknowable. In a short period of time, paleogenomics researchers dedicated to work in this region have brought our knowledge of prehistoric East Asia closer to that already established for longer-studied regions, such as Europe. These findings touch not just past populations and demographic movements, but also help explain linguistic dispersals, cultural networks, human response to climatic changes, and evolutionary adaptation. Ancient genomic evidence gives us an eyewitness account of prehistoric events. By characterizing the ancestry and admixture of ancient individuals, we can retrace the past movements and interactions of human lineages, including those which have disappeared and are thus invisible in present-day populations. This allows us to supply reliable responses to questions of "who?" to which, unlike "where?" and "when?" direct answers have long escaped paleoanthropological, osteological, and archeological interpretations.

In the emerging story, most East Asian populations can be traced back to an initial entry into East Asia of a primary ancestral lineage, ESEA, whose most basal representative currently appears to be the 40,000-year-old individual from Tianyuan, in northern China. Although its descendant lineages today occupy a large part of both northern and southern East Asia, from the inland to the coast, collective evidence indicates the main entry into East Asia may have been south of the Tibetan Plateau, primarily since the core populations of its nearest sister lineages are presently dispersed throughout southeastern Asia and surrounding islands; AASI is found primarily in South Asia, and AA in Australia and surrounding islands with Hòabìnhian ancestry coming to occupy Southeast Asia. Still, it is clear that some ancestry from modern human groups migrating north of the Tibetan Plateau and descendant from western Eurasian-branching lineages has become admixed within East Asian populations. Both ANS and ANE ancestry from Siberia has found its way into northeast East Asian populations, and has spread broadly due to subsequent population movements. Although this western Eurasian ancestry is found frequently in Mongolia and Xinjiang, as well as parts of Tibet, it has not become concentrated in most areas of East Asia.

ESEA ancestry then separates into distinct early branches, with Jōmon ancestry being found among the Japanese archipelago, and a deeply branching Tibetan ancestry of an unknown origin, both of which can be found admixed in modern descendants. The characterization of another deeply branching lineage, no longer found in present-day populations, at Longlin in Guangxi indicates that additional deeply branching human lineages may have developed that can only be detected through paleogenomic analysis. Within mainland East Asia, ESEA ancestry evolved into northern and southern lineages, with nEA in the north, distinct from the ANA ancestry appearing in the Amur Region by 14,000 years ago, ancient Fujian ancestry (sEA) in the southern coastal region, and ancient Guangxi in the southern inland. Some degree of admixture among these mainland lineages had already become evident prior to expansion of Yellow River Valley millet farmers to the Tibetan Plateau, West Liao River Valley, and Liangdong Peninsula beginning in the Early Neolithic.

ESEA lineages also appear beyond East Asia. Remnants of APS ancestry, an admixed profile of ESEA ANA and western Eurasian ANS lineages, are found in both ancient Siberian and present-day Native American populations, who also contain a branch of ANA ancestry dating to the LGM. Many present-day Siberians descend from neo-Siberian ancestry, which is predominantly ANA ancestry admixed with APS ancestry (Sikora *et al.* 2019). The Austronesian expansion has brought ESEA ancestry to a wide expanse of the world's islands, from Madagascar off the southeastern African coast to Polynesia as far as Rapa Nui (Ioannidis *et al.* 2020; Pierron *et al.* 2014). It now appears that the genetic origins of Austronesians may be found along the southern coast of China.

The origin and dispersal of both the Transeurasian and Sino-Tibetan language families are also more clearly understood due to ancient genomic results from East Asia. Transeurasian languages, which may have originated in northeastern East Asia within ANA populations, appear to have spread during the Neolithic from the West Liao River region northward and eastward into the Eastern Steppe forming the proto-Altaic branch, and into the Liaodong Peninsula to give rise to proto-Japano-Koreanic. Proto-Japonic is thought to have then arrived on the Japanese archipelago along with the expansion of rice agriculturalists from the Southern Korean Peninsula at the start of the Yayoi cultural period. The diffusion of Sino-Tibetan languages can be seen to follow the expansion of millet farmers out from the Yellow River Valley across East Asia, and westward into the Tibetan Plateau.

These population models, based on our current understanding of linguistic, archeological, and genetic evidence, are almost certainly over-simplifications of East Asia population history, and they continue to evolve and adapt as new discoveries come to light. Some major questions remain, the answers of which are sure to expose errors in our interpretations and bring about new questions. One large element missing from current models is a more precise understanding of the routes by which East Asia was populated. Some evidence suggests both coastal and inland routes, which may have left common traces of deeply branching ancestry along coastal populations related to Önge or Jōmon populations, but agreement on the source or timing of these signals has not yet reached a consensus. The identification of lost deeply branching "ghost" ancestries, such as those found in Longlin in Guangxi, or Tarim_EMBA in the Tarim Basin, is required to more accurately characterize later descendant populations, and so important work must be carried out to create a fuller catalog of the hidden corners of past genetic landscapes. An important example would be the identification of the people related to the source of the core Tibetan ancestry of the Tibetan Plateau. A denser map of Upper Paleolithic populations closer to the separation time of these deep branches will lead to a better understand of the factors behind the origin of the Jōmon, for example, and the reported relation of this ancestry with ANS. The same can be said for the earliest Tarim Basin and Hòabìnhian ancestries. Mainland genomes dating to the end of the LGM could help to better understand the process of the early north–south division revealed in East Asian genetics. Could this follow a simple distance by isolation model, established as new groups become more genetically isolated as they moved north following the LGM? Or does it underlie more complex movements?

One major gap stands out in this survey of Eastern Asia populations, that of early rice farmers from the Yangtze River Valley. The establishment of developed agricultural societies from prior rice harvesting practices is thought to rival that of the Yellow River in its age and impact, but to date there is a severe lack of available data to understand the populations behind this process. Identification of the pre-Neolithic groups inhabiting the lower Yangtze River may also supply new targets for investigating the mainland origins of the proto-Austronesions. Pre-Neolithic genetic information is also missing from Xinjiang and the Tibetan Plateau. In Xinjiang this could provide a time frame for the arrival of the ANE ancestors of the Tarim_EMBA ancestry, and may explain where they were during the period of genetic isolation leading to that particular genomic profile. Characterizing the groups who left behind several pre-LGM archeological sites on the Tibetan Plateau may allow insights into our views of modern human adaptation when faced with such a difficult altitude and climate. Archaic genomes from the same region might answer important questions about the range and population structure of altitude-adapted Denisovans, and perhaps better localize the source populations of the introgressed *EPAS1* allele.

Investigations into the population history of East Asia clearly have ample areas to explore, but given the wealth of results that have already been produced, ancient East Asian genomics can no longer be considered as a field in its infancy. The development of technological advances will improve the pace and scope of future research, and will be required to improve recovery of genetic information from challenging samples and regions. New avenues of ancient molecular study will also play an important role, including ancient proteomics, ancient oral microbiomes, and genetic analysis of sediments. Higher coverage of new and existing material using complete genomes recovered through shotgun or whole genome capture will also increase the types of information that can be extracted beyond the limits of the selected SNPs commonly used in capture panels, such as fine-scaled demographic structure and improved models of selection. Research is already underway attempting to fill in some of the empty spaces; some of these projects are sure to incorporate more advanced approaches. Just ten years from the first sequencing of a Pleistocene East Asian genome, the growing activity in East Asian ancient genomics research has added an enormous amount of information to our evolving understanding of human prehistory in East Asia. The ongoing focus of researchers ensures that the next ten years will bring still more surprises and challenges.

Glossary of Ancestries

AA – Australasian, one of three deeply branching East Asian lineages (with AASI and ESEA). AA includes modern-day Papuans and Aboriginal Australians.

AASI – Ancient Ancestral South Indian, one of three deeply branching East Asian lineages (with AA and ESEA). This South Asian hunter-gatherer ancestry is found primarily in present-day southern India and South Asia.

ANA – Ancient Northeast Asian ancestry appears to have been predominant throughout the Amur River Basin since the end of the LGM, stretching into southern Siberia, the West Liao River, and much of Mongolia. ANA ancestry is similar to that of some present-day groups still living in the Amur River region, where it has persisted for at least 14,000 years.

Ancient Fujian – Ancestry found in coastal southern East Asia from at least the Neolithic. It can be further differentiated as older Fujian_EN ancestry, as found in Qihe and Liangdao, and that of later Fujian_LN populations such as Tanshishan, which have a greater nEA component.

Ancient Guangxi – A distinct and early-branching ESEA lineage currently characterized from 11,000-year-old remains at Longlin in Guangxi. This ancestry was found in Paleolithic southern East Asian inland populations but no longer exists in unadmixed form.

ANE – Ancient North Eurasian ancestry. An important Paleolithic ancestry possibly descended from a primarily western Eurasian lineage similar to ANS. ANE was characterized from a 25,000-year-old individual near Lake Baikal in Siberia, and has contributed ancestry to populations both in northern Europe and the Americas. Presently extinct in unadmixed form, it was most recently documented as the major ancestral component of Bronze Age mummies from the Tarim Basin in Xinjiang (Tarim_EMBA1).

ANS – Ancient North Siberian ancestry was thought to have split from the lineage leading to western Eurasians 4,000–5,000 years after separating from that of eastern Eurasians, and later receiving roughly 20% ancestry from an East Asian lineage. It is the ancestry present at the 32,000-year-old Yana site of northern Siberia, and was one of two divergent ancestries found in northeastern Eurasia during the Upper Paleolithic, the other being Tianyuan-like. The 34,000-year-old individual from Salkhit Mongolia contained admixed ANS and Tianyuan ancestry.

APS – Ancient Paleo-Siberian ancestry, identified in a 10,000-year-old individual from the Kolyma River in Siberia and a 14,000-year-old individual (UKY) near Lake Baikal, can be modeled as admixture between mostly west Eurasian branching ANS-like ancestry, such as that found in Yana, and an East Asian lineage. The first Native American founding populations involved APS-like ancestry admixed with additional ANA lineages.

Austronesian – the populations that would colonize islands of the South West Pacific and Indian Oceans beginning some 4,000 years ago were thought to have an ancestry similar to the 3,000-year-old remains from Vanuatu. While this ancestry is similar to that of ancient southern East Asian coastal populations near Fujian, a more precise mainland source population has yet to be found.

BMAC – Originally characterized in individuals associated with the Central Asian Bronze Age Bactria-Margiana Archaeological Complex (BMAC) centered around the upper Amu Darya River, BMAC ancestry is found in EBA Xinjiang, and in southern Altai Chermurchek populations.

EAT – Early Ancient Tibetan ancestry is represented by the population at Zongri in the Tibetan Plateau, 5,000 years ago. Zongri5.1K is the closest example yet found to indigenous Tibetan Plateau ancestry prior to the Early to Middle Neolithic arrival of YR ancestry and other influences from outside the region, such as Inner Mongolia.

ESEA – East and Southeast Asian, one of three deeply branching East Asian lineages (with AA and AASI). This basal East Asian lineage is ancestral to most of the populations of East and Southeast Asia, including Tianyuan, nEA, sEA, ancient Guangxi, Austronesian, and Jomon.

Hòabìnhian – first identified from remains associated with the Hòabìnhian Cultural complex in Southeast Asia. This ancestry is thought to represent indigenous hunter-gatherer groups of this region, and perhaps also in southern East Asia, where it has been found admixed with various East Asian lineages as early as 8,000 years ago. Hòabìnhian ancestry is closely associated with present-day groups speaking Austroasiatic languages.

Jōmon – Jōmon ancestry is another early-branching ancestry from the ESEA lineage, having diverged roughly the same time as ancient Guangxi, and is found in Paleolithic populations from the Japanese archipelago up to 7,000 years ago (although the associated culture goes back to 16,000 BP).

nEA – northern East Asian ancestry is a broad term encompassing many northern East Asian groups, who have been genetically distinct from sEA groups since for at least 19,000 years. It designates the common northern East Asian ancestry found in ANA and YR ancestries, and in populations from areas such as Shandong, West Liao River, and Inner Mongolia.

Önge – A deeply divergent East Asian ancestry belonging to the AA lineage, with some shared genetic ancestry with Hòabìnhian. Found in present-day Andaman Islanders.

sEA – southern East Asian represents related ancestries belonging to ancient southern East Asian groups, distinguishing them from nEA. This includes ancient Fujian ancestry and that related to the Austronesians.

Tarim_EMBA – A Bronze Age occurrence of mostly ANE ancestry with a low ANA component similar to that found around Lake Baikal. Tarim_EMBA ancestry is found in the earlier Tarim Basin mummies, and shows signs of a genetic bottleneck and an extended isolation period.

Tianyuan – Tianyuan is a 40,000-year-old northern East Asian individual with a distinct ancestry that was once wide-spread across northern East Asia, including Mongolia and the Amur River region. It is the oldest East Asian ancestry identified and lasted at least 7,000 years before the last glacial period.

WSH – Western Steppe Herder ancestry describes that found associated with the EBA Afanasievo archeological culture of southern Siberia and later related western steppe cultures such as the MLBA Sintashta and Andronovo. Later MLBA WSH groups can be differentiated by the Afanasievo by the presence of Anatolian farmer ancestry, which is thought to have come from contact with the Corded Ware culture of Europe.

YR – Yellow River ancestry refers to that of the early agricultural communities of the Yellow River Valley. The Middle Neolithic YR_MN can be associated with the Yangshao archeological culture of the Central Plain, but is also found from the West Liao River to Inner Mongolia. The Late Neolithic YR_LN can be associated with the Longshan culture and is distinguished from the YR_MN by a higher southern East Asian component. The spread of Sino-Tibetan languages is thought to have accompanied the expansion of YR ancestry.

References

Abuduresule, I., Li, W., & Hu, X. (2007). 新疆罗布泊小河墓地2003年发掘简报 [A brief excavation report on Xiaohe graveyard located in Luobupo, Xinjiang Autonomous Region]. *Cultural Relics*, **10**(4), 42.

Adachi, N., Kakuda, T., Takahashi, R., Kanzawa-Kiriyama, H., & Shinoda, K. (2018). Ethnic derivation of the Ainu inferred from ancient mitochondrial DNA data. *American Journal of Physical Anthropology*, **165**(1), 139–148.

Adachi, N., Kanzawa-Kiriyama, H., Nara, T. et al. (2021). Ancient genomes from the initial Jomon period: New insights into the genetic history of the Japanese archipelago. *Anthropological Science*, **129**(1), 13–22.

Adachi, N., Shinoda, K., Umetsu, K. et al. (2011). Mitochondrial DNA analysis of Hokkaido Jomon skeletons: Remnants of archaic maternal lineages at the southwestern edge of former Beringia. *American Journal of Physical Anthropology*, **146**(3), 346–360.

Agadjanian, A. K., & Shunkov, M. V. (2018). Paleolithic man of Denisova cave and zoogeography of Pleistocene mammals of Northwestern Altai. *Paleontological Journal*, **52**(1), 66–89.

Aldenderfer, M. (2011). Peopling the Tibetan plateau: Insights from archaeology. *High Altitude Medicine & Biology*, **12**(2), 141–147.

Allen, E., Yu, Y., Yang, X. et al. (2022). Multidisciplinary lines of evidence reveal East/Northeast Asian origins of agriculturalist/pastoralist residents at a Han dynasty military outpost in ancient Xinjiang. *Frontiers in Ecology and Evolution*, **10**, 932004.

Allentoft, M. E., Collins, M., Harker, D. et al. (2012). The half-life of DNA in bone: Measuring decay kinetics in 158 dated fossils. *Proceedings of the Royal Society B: Biological Sciences*, **279**(1748), 4724–4733.

Allentoft, M. E., Sikora, M., Sjögren, K.-G. et al. (2015). Population genomics of Bronze Age Eurasia. *Nature*, **522**(7555), 167–172.

Anthony, D. W., & Ringe, D. (2015). The Indo-European homeland from linguistic and archaeological perspectives. *Annual Review of Linguistics*, **1** (1), 199–219.

Ávila-Arcos, M. C., Cappellini, E., Romero-Navarro, J. A. et al. (2011). Application and comparison of large-scale solution-based DNA capture-enrichment methods on ancient DNA. *Scientific Reports*, **1**(1), 74.

Bae, C. J., & Guyomarc'h, P. (2015). Potential contributions of Korean Pleistocene hominin fossils to palaeoanthropology: A view from Ryonggok Cave. *Asian Perspectives*, **54**(1), 31–57.

Bae, C. J., Wang, W., Zhao, J. et al. (2014). Modern human teeth from Late Pleistocene Luna Cave (Guangxi, China). *Quaternary International*, **354**, 169–183.

Baelz, E. von. (1911). Die Riu-Kiu-Insulaner, die Aino und andere Kaukasierahnliche Reste in Ostasien [Ryukyu Islanders, the Ainu, and other Caucasian-like remains in East Asia]. *Korrespondenz-Blatt Der Deutschen Gesellschaft Fur Anthropologie, Ethnologie Ind Urgeschichte*, **42**, 187–191.

Bailey, H. W. (1970). Saka studies: The ancient kingdom of Khotan. *Iran*, **8**, 65.

Barros Damgaard, P., Martiniano, R., Kamm, J. et al. (2018). The first horse herders and the impact of early Bronze Age steppe expansions into Asia. *Science*, **360**, eaar7711.

Bennett, E. A., Crevecoeur, I., Viola, B. et al. (2019). Morphology of the Denisovan phalanx closer to modern humans than to Neanderthals. *Science Advances*, **5**(9), eaaw3950.

Betts, A., Jia, P., & Abuduresule, I. (2019a). A new hypothesis for early Bronze Age cultural diversity in Xinjiang, China. *Archaeological Research in Asia*, **17**, 204–213.

Betts, A. V., Vicziany, M., Jia, P., & Castro, A. A. (Eds.). (2019b). *The Cultures of Ancient Xinjiang, Western China: Crossroads of the Silk Roads*, Summertown, Oxford: Archaeopress.

Blench, R., & Post, M. (2014). Rethinking Sino-Tibetan phylogeny from the perspective of North East Indian languages. In N. Hill & T. Owen-Smith, eds., *Trans-Himalayan linguistics*, Berlin: De Gruyter Mouton, pp. 71–104.

Boer, E., Yang, M., Kawagoe, A., & Barnes, G. (2020). Japan considered from the hypothesis of farmer/language spread. *Evolutionary Human Sciences*, **2**, 13.

Brace, S., Diekmann, Y., Booth, T. J. et al. (2019). Ancient genomes indicate population replacement in Early Neolithic Britain. *Nature Ecology & Evolution*, **3**(5), 765–771.

Briggs, A. W., Stenzel, U., Johnson, P. L. et al. (2007). Patterns of damage in genomic DNA sequences from a Neandertal. *Proceedings of the National Academy of Sciences*, **104**, 14616–21.

Briggs, A. W., Stenzel, U., Meyer, M. et al. (2010). Removal of deaminated cytosines and detection of in vivo methylation in ancient DNA. *Nucleic Acids Research*, **38**(6), e87–e87.

Browning, S. R., Browning, B. L., Zhou, Y., Tucci, S., & Akey, J. M. (2018). Analysis of human sequence data reveals two pulses of archaic Denisovan admixture. *Cell*, **173**(1), 53–61.e9.

Bryk, J., Hardouin, E., Pugach, I. et al. (2008). Positive selection in East Asians for an EDAR Allele that enhances NF-κB activation. *PLoS ONE*, **3**(5), e2209.

Cai, Y., Fu, W., Cai, D. et al. (2020). Ancient genomes reveal the evolutionary history and origin of cashmere-producing goats in China. *Molecular Biology and Evolution*, **37**(7), 2099–2109.

Chang, K. C. (1989). The Neolithic Taiwan Strait. *Archeology*, **6**, 541–550, 569.

Chen, F., Welker, F., Shen, C.-C. et al. (2019). A late middle Pleistocene Denisovan mandible from the Tibetan Plateau. *Nature*, **569**(7756), 409–412.

Chi, Z., & Festa, M. (2020). Archaeological research in the Ili Region: A review. *Asian Perspectives*, **59**(2), 338–384.

Cooke, N. P., Mattiangeli, V., Cassidy, L. M. et al. (2021). Ancient genomics reveals tripartite origins of Japanese populations. *Science Advances*, *7*, eabh2419.

Crawford, G. W. (2011). Advances in understanding early agriculture in Japan. *Current Anthropology*, **52**(S4), S331–S345.

Crawford, G. W., Chen, X., & Wang, J. (2006). 山东济南长清区月庄遗址发现后李文化时期的炭化稻 [Houli culture rice from the Yuezhuang site, Jinan]. *East Asia Archeology*, **3**, 247–251.

Crawford, G. W., & Lee, G.-A. (2003). Agricultural origins in the Korean Peninsula. *Antiquity*, **77**(295), 87–95.

Cui, Y., Zhang, F., Ma, P. et al. (2020). Bioarchaeological perspective on the expansion of Transeurasian languages in Neolithic Amur River basin. *Evolutionary Human Sciences*, **2**, e15.

Dabney, J., Meyer, M., & Paabo, S. (2013). Ancient DNA damage. *Cold Spring Harbor Perspectives in Biology*, **5**(7), a012567–a012567.

Dai, J., Cai, X., Jin, J. et al. (2021). Earliest arrival of millet in the South China coast dating back to 5,500 years ago. *Journal of Archaeological Science*, **129**, 105356.

Damgaard, P. B., Marchi, N., Rasmussen, S. et al. (2018). 137 ancient human genomes from across the Eurasian steppes. *Nature*, **557**, 369–374.

Dashtseveg, T., Dorjpurev, K., & Myagmar, E. (2013). Bronze age graves in the Delgerkhaan mountain area of Eastern Mongolia and the Ulaanzuukh culture. *Asian Archaeology*, **2**, 40–49.

Deagle, B. E., Eveson, J. P., & Jarman, S. N. (2006). Quantification of damage in DNA recovered from highly degraded samples – a case study on DNA in faeces. *Frontiers in Zoology*, **3**(1), 11.

Demattè, P. (2010). The Origins of Chinese writing: The Neolithic evidence. *Cambridge Archaeological Journal*, **20**(2), 211–228.

Demeter, F., Zanolli, C., Westaway, K. E. et al. (2022). A middle Pleistocene Denisovan molar from the Annamite chain of northern Laos. *Nature Communications*, **13**(1), 2557.

Détroit, F., Mijares, A. S., Corny, J. et al. (2019). A new species of Homo from the Late Pleistocene of the Philippines. *Nature*, **568**(7751), 181–186.

Dong, W. (2016). Biochronological framework of Homo erectus horizons in China. *Quaternary International*, **400**, 47–57.

Douka, K., Slon, V., Jacobs, Z. et al. (2019). Age estimates for hominin fossils and the onset of the Upper Palaeolithic at Denisova Cave. *Nature*, **565**(7741), 640–644.

Doumani Dupuy, P. N., Tabaldiev, K., & Matuzeviciute, G. M. (2023). A wooly way? Fiber technologies and cultures 3,000-years-ago along the Inner Asian mountain corridor. *Frontiers in Ecology and Evolution*, **10**, 1070775.

Fei, X. (2017). The formation and development of the Chinese nation with multi-ethnic groups. *International Journal of Anthropology and Ethnology*, **1**(1), 1.

Fernández-Crespo, T., & de-la-Rúa, C. (2015). Demographic evidence of selective burial in megalithic graves of northern Spain. *Journal of Archaeological Science*, **53**, 604–617.

Frachetti, M. D. (2008). *Pastoralist Landscapes and Social Interaction in Bronze Age Eurasia*, Berkeley: University of California Press.

Fu, Q., Hajdinjak, M., Moldovan, O. T. et al. (2015). An early modern human from Romania with a recent Neanderthal ancestor. *Nature*, **524**(7564), 216–219.

Fu, Q., Li, H., Moorjani, P. et al. (2014). Genome sequence of a 45,000-year-old modern human from western Siberia. *Nature*, **514**(7523), 445–449.

Fu, Q., Meyer, M., Gao, X. et al. (2013). DNA analysis of an early modern human from Tianyuan Cave, China. *Proceedings of the National Academy of Sciences*, **110**(6), 2223–2227.

Gakuhari, T., Nakagome, S., Rasmussen, S. et al. (2020). Ancient Jomon genome sequence analysis sheds light on migration patterns of early East Asian populations. *Communications Biology*, **3**(1), 437.

Gamba, C., Jones, E. R., Teasdale, M. D. et al. (2014). Genome flux and stasis in a five millennium transect of European prehistory. *Nature Communications*, **5**(1), 5257.

Gao, X., Zhou, Z. Y., & Guan, Y. (2008). 青藏高原边缘地区晚更新世人类遗存与生存模式 [Human cultural remains and adaptation strategies in the Tibetan Plateau margin region in the late Pleistocene]. *Quaternary Science*, **28**, 969–977.

Gladyshev, S. A., Olsen, J. W., Tabarev, A. V., & Kuzmin, Y. V. (2010). Chronology and periodization of Upper Paleolithic sites in Mongolia. *Archaeology, Ethnology and Anthropology of Eurasia*, **38**(3), 33–40.

Gnecchi-Ruscone, G. A., Jeong, C., De Fanti, S. et al. (2017). The genomic landscape of Nepalese Tibeto-Burmans reveals new insights into the recent peopling of Southern Himalayas. *Scientific Reports*, **7**(1), 15512.

Gnecchi-Ruscone, G. A., Khussainova, E., Kahbatkyzy, N. et al. (2021). Ancient genomic time transect from the Central Asian Steppe unravels the history of the Scythians. *Science Advances*, **7**(13), eabe4414.

Green, R. E., Krause, J., Briggs, A. W. et al. (2010). A draft sequence of the Neandertal genome. *Science*, **328**(5979), 710–722.

Green, R. E., Krause, J., Ptak, S. E. et al. (2006). Analysis of one million base pairs of Neanderthal DNA. *Nature*, **444**(7117), 330–336.

Green, R. E., Malaspinas, A.-S., Krause, J. et al. (2008). A complete Neandertal mitochondrial genome sequence determined by high-throughput sequencing. *Cell*, **134**(3), 416–426.

Habu, J. (2004). *Ancient Jomon of Japan*, Cambridge: Cambridge University Press.

Habu, J. (2010). Seafaring and the development of cultural complexity in Northeast Asia: Evidence from the Japanese archipelago. In A. Anderson, J. H. Barrett, & K. V. Boyle, eds., *The Global Origins and Development of Seafaring*, Cambridge: McDonald Institute for Archaeological Research Cambridge, pp. 159–170.

Hajdinjak, M., Mafessoni, F., Skov, L. et al. (2021). Initial Upper Palaeolithic humans in Europe had recent Neanderthal ancestry. *Nature*, **592**(7853), 253–257.

Hammer, M. F., Karafet, T. M., Park, H. et al. (2006). Dual origins of the Japanese: Common ground for hunter-gatherer and farmer Y chromosomes. *Journal of Human Genetics*, **51**(1), 47–58.

Han, J. (2012). “The Painted Pottery Road” and early Sino-Western cultural exchanges. *Anabasis*, **3**, 25–42.

Han, K. (1999). 古新疆居民种族亲和力的体质人类学研究 [Physical Anthro pological Studies on the Racial Affinities of the Inhabitants of Ancient Xinjiang]. In B. H. Wang, ed., 新疆古尸: 古代新疆居民及其文化 *[The Ancient Corpses of Xinjiang: the Peoples of Ancient Xinjiang and their Culture]*, Urumqi: Xinjiang People’s Publishing House, pp. 224–241.

Hanihara, K. (1991). Dual structure model for the population history of the Japanese. *Japan Review*, **2**, 1–33.

Hanihara, T., & Ishida, H. (2009). Regional differences in craniofacial diversity and the population history of Jomon Japan. *American Journal of Physical Anthropology*, **139**(3), 311–322.

Hansen, H. B., Damgaard, P. B., Margaryan, A. et al. (2017). Comparing ancient DNA preservation in petrous bone and tooth cementum. *PLoS ONE*, **12**(1), e0170940.

He, G., Wang, M., Zou, X. et al. (2021). Peopling history of the Tibetan plateau and multiple waves of admixture of Tibetans inferred from both ancient and modern genome-wide data. *Frontiers in Genetics*, **12**, 1634.

Hemphill, B. E., & Mallory, J. P. (2004). Horse-mounted invaders from the Russo-Kazakh steppe or agricultural colonists from western Central Asia? A craniometric investigation of the Bronze Age settlement of Xinjiang. *American Journal of Physical Anthropology*, **124**, 199–222.

Hou, G., Xu, C. J., Lu, C. Q., Chen, Q., & Lancuo, Z. (2019). The environmental background of Yangshao culture expansion in the mid-Holocene. *Geographical Research*, **02**, 437–444.

Hu, Y., Wang, S., Luan, F., Wang, C., & Richards, M. P. (2008). Stable isotope analysis of humans from Xiaojingshan site: Implications for understanding the origin of millet agriculture in China. *Journal of Archaeological Science*, **35**(11), 2960–2965.

Hublin, J.-J. (2021). How old are the oldest *Homo sapiens* in Far East Asia? *Proceedings of the National Academy of Sciences*, **118**(10), e2101173118.

Huerta-Sánchez, E., Jin, X., Asan et al. (2014). Altitude adaptation in Tibetans caused by introgression of Denisovan-like DNA. *Nature*, **512**(7513), 194–197.

Ioannidis, A. G., Blanco-Portillo, J., Sandoval, K. et al. (2020). Native American gene flow into Polynesia predating Easter Island settlement. *Nature*, **583**(7817), 572–577.

Janz, L., Odsuren, D., & Bukhchuluun, D. (2017). Transitions in palaeoecology and technology: Hunter-Gatherers and early herders in the Gobi desert. *Journal of World Prehistory*, **30**(1), 1–80.

Japanese Archipelago Human Population Genetics Consortium. (2012). The history of human populations in the Japanese Archipelago inferred from genome-wide SNP data with a special reference to the Ainu and the Ryukyuan populations. *Journal of Human Genetics*, **57**(12), 787–795.

Jeong, C., Nakagome, S., & Di Rienzo, A. (2016). Deep history of East Asian populations revealed through genetic analysis of the Ainu. *Genetics*, **202**(1), 261–272.

Jeong, C., Peter, B. M., Basnyat, B. et al. (2017). A longitudinal cline characterizes the genetic structure of human populations in the Tibetan plateau. *PLoS ONE*, **12**(4), e0175885.

Jeong, C., Wang, K., Wilkin, S. et al. (2020). A dynamic 6,000-year genetic history of Eurasia's Eastern steppe. *Cell*, **183**(4), 890–904.e29.

Ji, X., Kuman, K., Clarke, R. J. et al. (2016). The oldest Hoabinhian technocomplex in Asia (43.5 ka) at Xiaodong rockshelter, Yunnan Province, southwest China. *Quaternary International*, **400**, 166–174.

Jia, P. W., Betts, A., Cong, D., Jia, X., & Dupuy, P. D. (2017). Adunqiaolu: New evidence for the Andronovo in Xinjiang, China. *Antiquity*, **91**(357), 621–639.

Jia, X., Sun, Y., Wang, L. et al. (2016). The transition of human subsistence strategies in relation to climate change during the Bronze Age in the West Liao River Basin, Northeast China. *The Holocene*, **26**(5), 781–789.

Jin, G., Wagner, M., Tarasov, P. E., Wang, F., & Liu, Y. (2016). Archaeobotanical records of Middle and Late Neolithic agriculture from Shandong Province, East China, and a major change in regional subsistence during the Dawenkou Culture. *The Holocene*, **26**(10), 1605–1615.

Jinam, T. A., Kanzawa-Kiriyama, H., & Saitou, N. (2015). Human genetic diversity in the Japanese Archipelago: Dual structure and beyond. *Genes & Genetic Systems*, **90**(3), 147–152.

Kamberov, Y. G., Wang, S., Tan, J. et al. (2013). Modeling recent human evolution in mice by expression of a selected EDAR variant. *Cell*, **152**(4), 691–702.

Kanzawa-Kiriyama, H., Jinam, T. A., Kawai, Y. et al. (2019). Late Jomon male and female genome sequences from the Funadomari site in Hokkaido, Japan. *Anthropological Science*, **127**(2), 83–108.

Kanzawa-Kiriyama, H., Kryukov, K., Jinam, T. A. et al. (2017). A partial nuclear genome of the Jomons who lived 3000 years ago in Fukushima, Japan. *Journal of Human Genetics*, **62**(2), 213–221.

Kanzawa-Kiriyama, H., Saso, A., Suwa, G., & Saitou, N. (2013). Ancient mitochondrial DNA sequences of Jomon teeth samples from Sanganji, Tohoku district, Japan. *Anthropological Science*, **121**(2), 89–103.

Kassian, A. S., Zhivlov, M., Starostin, G. et al. (2021). Rapid radiation of the inner Indo-European languages: An advanced approach to Indo-European lexicostatistics. *Linguistics*, **59**(4), 949–979.

Kim, J., Jeon, S., Choi, J.-P. et al. (2020). The origin and composition of Korean ethnicity analyzed by ancient and present-day Genome sequences. *Genome Biology and Evolution*, **12**(5), 553–565.

Kim, Y. J., & Park, S. (2017). Tectonic traditions in ancient Chinese architecture, and their development. *Journal of Asian Architecture and Building Engineering*, **16**(1), 31–38.

Kistler, L., Ware, R., Smith, O., Collins, M., & Allaby, R. G. (2017). A new model for ancient DNA decay based on paleogenomic meta-analysis. *Nucleic Acids Research*, **45**(11), 6310–6320.

Ko, A. M.-S., Chen, C.-Y., Fu, Q. et al. (2014). Early Austronesians: Into and out of Taiwan. *The American Journal of Human Genetics*, **94**(3), 426–436.

Kolobova, K. A., Roberts, R. G., Chabai, V. P. et al. (2020). Archaeological evidence for two separate dispersals of Neanderthals into southern Siberia. *Proceedings of the National Academy of Sciences*, **117**(6), 2879–2885.

Kovalev, A. A. (2016). Гравированные Каменные Пластинки Из Чемурчекского Ритуального Комплекса Хар Чулуут 1 И Гипотеза

Западноевропейского Происхождения Чемурчекского Феномена [Engraved Stone Plaques from the Ritual Complex of Khar Chuluut 1 and the Hypothesis of Western European Origin of Chemurchek (Qiemuerqieke) Phenomenon]. In V. V. Bobrov, ed., *Archaeological Heritage of Siberia and Central Asia (Problems of Interpretation and Preservation): proceedings of the International Conference*, Kemerovo, Russia: Kuzbassvuzizdat, pp. 136–143.

Kumar, V., Wang, W., Zhang, J. et al. (2022). Bronze and Iron Age population movements underlie Xinjiang population history. *Science*, **376**(6588), 62–69.

Kuz/mina, E. E., & Mallory, J. P. (2007). *The origin of the Indo-Iranians*, Leiden, the Netherlands: Brill.

Kuzmin, Y. V. (2013). The beginnings of prehistoric agriculture in the Russian Far East: Current evidence and concepts. *Documenta Praehistorica*, **40**, 1–12.

Kuzmin, Y. V. (2017). The origins of pottery in East Asia and neighboring regions: An analysis based on radiocarbon data. *Quaternary International*, **441**, 29–35.

Kuzmina, E. E. (1998). Cultural connections of the Tarim Basin people and pastoralists of the Asian steppes in the Bronze Age. *The Bronze Age and Early Iron Age Peoples of Eastern Central Asia*, **1**, 63–93.

Lancuo, Z., Hou, G., Xu, C. et al. (2023). Simulation of exchange routes on the Qinghai-Tibetan Plateau shows succession from the neolithic to the bronze age and strong control of the physical environment and production mode. *Frontiers in Earth Science*, **10**, 1079055.

Larena, M., McKenna, J., Sanchez-Quinto, F. et al. (2021a). Philippine Ayta possess the highest level of Denisovan ancestry in the world. *Current Biology*, **31**(19), 4219–4230.e10.

Larena, M., Sanchez-Quinto, F., Sjödin, P. et al. (2021b). Multiple migrations to the Philippines during the last 50,000 years. *Proceedings of the National Academy of Sciences*, **118**(13), e2026132118.

Lee, J., Miller, B. K., Bayarsaikhan, J. et al. (2023). Genetic population structure of the Xiongnu Empire at imperial and local scales. *Science Advances*, **9** (15), eadf3904.

Li, C., Li, H., Cui, Y. et al. (2010). Evidence that a West-East admixed population lived in the Tarim Basin as early as the early Bronze Age. *BMC Biology*, **8**(1), 15.

Li, C., Ning, C., Hagelberg, E. et al. (2015). Analysis of ancient human mitochondrial DNA from the Xiaohe cemetery: Insights into prehistoric population movements in the Tarim Basin, China. *BMC Genetics*, **16**, 78.

Li, F., Vanwezer, N., Boivin, N. et al. (2019). Heading north: Late Pleistocene environments and human dispersals in central and eastern Asia. *PLoS ONE*, **14**(5), e0216433.

Li, J. W. (2015). *Genetic Diversity Research of Ancient Human Remains in the Central Plains in Yangshao Period*, Changchun: Jilin University.

Li, K., Gao, W., Wu, L. et al. (2021). Spatial expansion of human settlement during the Longshan period (~4.5—~3.9 ka BP) and its hydroclimatic contexts in the lower Yellow River floodplain, Eastern China. *Land*, **10**(7), 712.

Li, K., Qin, X., Yang, X. et al. (2018). Human activity during the late Pleistocene in the Lop Nur region, northwest China: Evidence from a buried stone artifact. *Science China Earth Sciences*, **61**(11), 1659–1668.

Li, T. J. (2019). 中原地区仰韶文化时期古代人类遗骸的遗传多态性研究 *[Genomic Study of the Ancient Populations from the period of YangShao to LongShan culture in Central Plain] (Thesis)*, Changchun: Jilin University.

Li, T., Ning, C., Zhushchikhovskaya, I. S. et al. (2020). Millet agriculture dispersed from Northeast China to the Russian Far East: Integrating archaeology, genetics, and linguistics. *Archaeological Research in Asia*, **22**, 100177.

Li, Z.-Y., Wu, X.-J., Zhou, L.-P. et al. (2017). Late Pleistocene archaic human crania from Xuchang, China. *Science*, **355**(6328), 969–972.

Librado, P., Khan, N., Fages, A. et al. (2021). The origins and spread of domestic horses from the Western Eurasian steppes. *Nature*, **598**(7882), 634–640.

Lipson, M., Cheronet, O., Mallick, S. et al. (2018). Ancient genomes document multiple waves of migration in Southeast Asian prehistory. *Science*, **361** (6397), 92–95.

Lipson, M., & Reich, D. (2017). A working model of the deep relationships of diverse modern human genetic lineages outside of Africa. *Molecular Biology and Evolution*, **34**(4), 889–902.

Liu, C. J., & Kong, Z. C. (2004). 粟、黍籽粒的形态比较及其在考古鉴定中的意义 [The morphological comparison of grains between foxtail and broomcorn millet and its application for identification in archaeology remains]. *Kaogu (Archeology)*, **3**, 76–83.

Liu, C.-C., Witonsky, D., Gosling, A. et al. (2022). Ancient genomes from the Himalayas illuminate the genetic history of Tibetans and their Tibeto-Burman speaking neighbors. *Nature Communications*, **13**(1), 1203.

Liu, J., Zeng, W., Sun, B. et al. (2021). Maternal genetic structure in ancient Shandong between 9500 and 1800 years ago. *Science Bulletin*, **66**(11), 1129–1135.

Liu, L., & Chen, X. C. (2017). *The Archaeology of China: From the Late Paleolithic to the Early Bronze Age*, Shanghai: SDX Joint.

Liu, W., Martinón-Torres, M., Cai, Y. et al. (2015). The earliest unequivocally modern humans in southern China. *Nature*, **526**(7575), 696–699.

Lu, D., Lou, H., Yuan, K. et al. (2016). Ancestral origins and genetic history of Tibetan highlanders. *The American Journal of Human Genetics*, **99**(3), 580–594.

Lu, H. (2023). Local millet farming and permanent occupation on the Tibetan Plateau. *Science China Earth Sciences*, **66**(2), 430–434.

Lu, H., Zhang, J., Liu, K. et al. (2009). Earliest domestication of common millet (*Panicum miliaceum*) in East Asia extended to 10,000 years ago. *Proceedings of the National Academy of Sciences*, **106**(18), 7367–7372.

Lu, M., Chen, L., Wang, J. et al. (2019). A brief history of wheat utilization in China. *Frontiers of Agricultural Science and Engineering*, **6**(3), 288.

Lutaenko, K. A., Zhushchikhovskaya, I. S., Mikishin, Y. A., & Popov, A. N. (2007). Mid-Holocene climatic changes and cultural dynamics in the basin of the Sea of Japan and adjacent areas. In D. G. Anderson, K. Maasch, & D. H. Sandweiss, eds., *Climate Change and Cultural Dynamics*, New York: Elsevier, pp. 331–406.

Mallory, J. P., & Mair, V. H. (2000). *The Tarim Mummies*, London: Thames & Hudson.

Mao, X., Zhang, H., Qiao, S. et al. (2021). The deep population history of northern East Asia from the Late Pleistocene to the Holocene. *Cell*, **184**(12), 3256–3266.e13.

Massilani, D., Skov, L., Hajdinjak, M. et al. (2020). Denisovan ancestry and population history of early East Asians. *Science*, **370**(6516), 579–583.

Mathieson, I., Lazaridis, I., Rohland, N. et al. (2015). Genome-wide patterns of selection in 230 ancient Eurasians. *Nature*, **528**(7583), 499–503.

Matisoff, J. A. (1991). Sino-Tibetan linguistics: Present state and future prospects. *Annual Review of Anthropology*, **20**(1), 469–504.

Matsumura, H., Hung, H., Higham, C. et al. (2019). Craniometrics reveal "two layers" of prehistoric human dispersal in Eastern Eurasia. *Scientific Reports*, **9**(1), 1451.

Matsumura, H., & Oxenham, M. F. (2014). Demographic transitions and migration in prehistoric East/Southeast Asia through the lens of nonmetric dental traits: Transition and migration In East/Southeast Asia. *American Journal of Physical Anthropology*, **155**(1), 45–65.

McColl, H., Racimo, F., Vinner, L. et al. (2018). The prehistoric peopling of Southeast Asia. *Science*, **361**(6397), 88–92.

Miao, B., Liu, Y., Gu, W. et al. (2021). Maternal genetic structure of a neolithic population of the Yangshao culture. *Journal of Genetics and Genomics*, **48** (8), 746–750.

Miller, B. K. (2024). *Xiongnu: The World's First Nomadic Empire*, New York: Oxford University Press.

Miller, N. F., Spengler, R. N., & Frachetti, M. (2016). Millet cultivation across Eurasia: Origins, spread, and the influence of seasonal climate. *The Holocene*, **26**(10), 1566–1575.

Millward, A. J. (2007). *Eurasian Crossroads : A History of Xinjiang*, Columbia University Press.

Miyamoto, K. (2019). The spread of rice agriculture during the Yayoi Period: From the Shandong Peninsula to the Japanese Archipelago via the Korean Peninsula. *Japanese Journal of Archeology*, **6**(2), 109–124.

Miyamoto, K. (2022). The emergence of "Transeurasian" language families in Northeast Asia as viewed from archaeological evidence. *Evolutionary Human Sciences*, **4**, e3.

Mizoguchi, K. (2002). *An Archaeological History of Japan: 30,000 B.C. to A.D. 700*, Philadelphia: University of Pennsylvania Press.

Mizuno, F., Gojobori, J., Kumagai, M. et al. (2021). Population dynamics in the Japanese Archipelago since the Pleistocene revealed by the complete mitochondrial genome sequences. *Scientific Reports*, **11**(1), 12018.

Moreno-Mayar, J. V., Potter, B. A., Vinner, L. et al. (2018). Terminal Pleistocene Alaskan genome reveals first founding population of Native Americans. *Nature*, **553**(7687), 203–207.

Nakagawa, R., Doi, N., Nishioka, Y. et al. (2010). Pleistocene human remains from Shiraho-Saonetabaru Cave on Ishigaki Island, Okinawa, Japan, and their radiocarbon dating. *Anthropological Science*, **118**(3), 173–183.

Nakamura, T., Taniguchi, Y., Tsuji, S., & Oda, H. (2001). Radiocarbon dating of Charred residues on the earliest pottery in Japan. *Radiocarbon*, **43**(2B), 1129–1138.

Narasimhan, V. M., Patterson, N., Moorjani, P. et al. (2019). The formation of human populations in South and Central Asia. *Science*, **365**(6457), eaat7487.

Ning, C., Fernandes, D., Changmai, P. et al. (2020a). The genomic formation of First American ancestors in East and Northeast Asia. *BioRxiv*.

Ning, C., Li, T., Wang, K. et al. (2020b). Ancient genomes from northern China suggest links between subsistence changes and human migration. *Nature Communications*, **11**(1), 2700.

Ning, C., Wang, C. C., Gao, S. et al. (2019). Ancient genomes reveal Yamnaya-related ancestry and a potential source of Indo-European speakers in Iron Age Tianshan. *Current Biology*, **29**, 2526–2532.

Noonan, J. P., Coop, G., Kudaravalli, S. et al. (2006). Sequencing and analysis of Neanderthal genomic DNA. *Science*, **314**(5802), 1113–1118.

Ohshima, K. (1990). 第四紀後期の海峡形成史 [The history of straits around the Japanese Islands in the late-quaternary]. *The Quaternary Research (Daiyonki-Kenkyu)*, **29**(3), 193–208.

Ono, Y. (1990). 北の陸橋 [The northern landbridge of Japan]. *The Quaternary Research (Daiyonki-Kenkyu)*, **29**(3), 183–192.

Osada, N., & Kawai, Y. (2021). Exploring models of human migration to the Japanese archipelago using genome-wide genetic data. *Anthropological Science*, **129**(1), 45–58.

Patterson, N., Moorjani, P., Luo, Y. et al. (2012). Ancient admixture in human history. *Genetics*, **192**(3), 1065–1093.

Pearson, R. (2006). Jomon hot spot: Increasing sedentism in south-western Japan in the Incipient Jomon (14,000–9250 cal. BC) and Earliest Jomon (9250–5300 cal. BC) periods. *World Archaeology*, **38**(2), 239–258.

Peng, F., Lin, S. C., Patania, I. et al. (2020). A chronological model for the Late Paleolithic at Shuidonggou locality 2, North China. *PLoS ONE*, **15**(5), e0232682.

Peng, Y., Yang, Z., Zhang, H. et al. (2011). Genetic variations in Tibetan populations and high-altitude adaptation at the Himalayas. *Molecular Biology and Evolution*, **28**(2), 1075–1081.

Peter, B. M., Huerta-Sanchez, E., & Nielsen, R. (2012). Distinguishing between selective sweeps from standing variation and from a De Novo mutation. *PLoS Genetics*, **8**(10), e1003011.

Peyrot, M. (2017). Tocharian: An Indo-European language from China. In J. M. Kelder, S. P. L de Jong, & A. Mouret, eds., *Aspects of Globalisation. Mobility, Exchange and the Development of Multi-Cultural States*, Leiden: LURIS, pp. 12–17.

Pierron, D., Razafindrazaka, H., Pagani, L. et al. (2014). Genome-wide evidence of Austronesian–Bantu admixture and cultural reversion in a hunter-gatherer group of Madagascar. *Proceedings of the National Academy of Sciences*, **111**(3), 936–941.

Popov, A. N., Tabarev, A. V., & Mikishin, Y. A. (2014). Neolithization and ancient landscapes in southern Primorye, Russian Far East. *Journal of World Prehistory*, **27**(3–4), 247–261.

Prüfer, K. (2018). snpAD: An ancient DNA genotype caller. *Bioinformatics*, **34** (24), 4165–4171.

Prüfer, K., Posth, C., Yu, H. et al. (2021). A genome sequence from a modern human skull over 45,000 years old from Zlatý kůň in Czechia. *Nature Ecology & Evolution*, **5**(6), 820–825.

Pruvost, M., Schwarz, R., Correia, V. B. et al. (2007). Freshly excavated fossil bones are best for amplification of ancient DNA. *Proc Natl Acad Sci U S A*, **104**, 739–44.

Qi, X., Cui, C., Peng, Y. et al. (2013). Genetic evidence of paleolithic colonization and neolithic expansion of modern humans on the Tibetan plateau. *Molecular Biology and Evolution*, **30**(8), 1761–1778.

Qiu, Q., Wang, L., Wang, K. et al. (2015). Yak whole-genome resequencing reveals domestication signatures and prehistoric population expansions. *Nature Communications*, **6**(1), 10283.

Raghavan, M., Skoglund, P., Graf, K. E. et al. (2014). Upper Palaeolithic Siberian genome reveals dual ancestry of Native Americans. *Nature*, **505** (7481), 87–91.

Rasmussen, S. O., Bigler, M., Blockley, S. P. et al. (2014). A stratigraphic framework for abrupt climatic changes during the Last Glacial period based on three synchronized Greenland ice-core records: Refining and extending the INTIMATE event stratigraphy. *Quaternary Science Reviews*, **106**, 14–28.

Reich, D., Green, R. E., Kircher, M. et al. (2010). Genetic history of an archaic hominin group from Denisova Cave in Siberia. *Nature*, **468**(7327), 1053–1060.

Reich, D., Patterson, N., Kircher, M. et al. (2011). Denisova admixture and the first modern human dispersals into Southeast Asia and Oceania. *American Journal of Human Genetics*, **89**(4), 516–528.

Ren, S.-N., & Wu, Y.-L. (2010). 中国考古学·新石器时代卷 *[Chinese Archaeology: Neolithic Volume]*, Beijing: China Social Sciences Press.

Rizal, Y., Westaway, K. E., Zaim, Y. et al. (2020). Last appearance of Homo erectus at Ngandong, Java, 117,000–108,000 years ago. *Nature*, **577**(7790), 381–385.

Robbeets, M., Bouckaert, R., Conte, M. et al. (2021). Triangulation supports agricultural spread of the Transeurasian languages. *Nature*, **599**(7886), 616–621.

Rohland, N., Harney, E., Mallick, S., Nordenfelt, S., & Reich, D. (2015). Partial uracil–DNA–glycosylase treatment for screening of ancient DNA. *Philosophical Transactions of the Royal Society B: Biological Sciences*, **370**(1660), 20130624.

Rybin, E. P., Paine, C. H., Khatsenovich, A. M. et al. (2020). A new Upper Paleolithic occupation at the site of Tolbor-21 (Mongolia): Site formation, human behavior and implications for the regional sequence. *Quaternary International*, **559**, 133–149.

Sagart, L., Blench, R., & Sanchez-Mazas, A. (2005). *The Peopling of East Asia: Putting Together Archaeology, Linguistics and Genetics*, London: RoutledgeCurzon.

Sagart, L., Hsu, T.-F., Tsai, Y.-C. et al. (2018). A northern Chinese origin of Austronesian agriculture: New evidence on traditional Formosan cereals. *Rice*, **11**(1), 57.

Sagart, L., Jacques, G., Lai, Y., . . . List, J.-M. (2019). Dated language phylogenies shed light on the ancestry of Sino-Tibetan. *Proceedings of the National Academy of Sciences*, **116**(21), 10317–10322.

Sato, T., Nakagome, S., Watanabe, C. et al. (2014). Genome-wide SNP analysis reveals population structure and demographic history of the Ryukyu Islanders in the Southern part of the Japanese archipelago. *Molecular Biology and Evolution*, **31**(11), 2929–2940.

Seguin-Orlando, A., Korneliussen, T. S., Sikora, M. et al. (2014). Genomic structure in Europeans dating back at least 36,200 years. *Science*, **346**(6213), 1113–1118.

Shen, G., Wu, X., Wang, Q. et al. (2013). Mass spectrometric U-series dating of Huanglong Cave in Hubei Province, central China: Evidence for early presence of modern humans in eastern Asia. *Journal of Human Evolution*, **65**(2), 162–167.

Shi, H., Zhong, H., Peng, Y. et al. (2008). Y chromosome evidence of earliest modern human settlement in East Asia and multiple origins of Tibetan and Japanese populations. *BMC Biology*, **6**(1), 45.

Shoda, S., Lucquin, A., Yanshina, O. et al. (2020). Late Glacial hunter-gatherer pottery in the Russian Far East: Indications of diversity in origins and use. *Quaternary Science Reviews*, **229**, 106124.

Sikora, M., Pitulko, V. V., Sousa, V. C. et al. (2019). The population history of northeastern Siberia since the Pleistocene. *Nature*, **570**(7760), 182–188.

Siska, V., Jones, E. R., Jeon, S. et al. (2017). Genome-wide data from two early Neolithic East Asian individuals dating to 7700 years ago. *Science Advances*, **3**(2), e1601877.

Skoglund, P., Posth, C., Sirak, K. et al. (2016). Genomic insights into the peopling of the Southwest pacific. *Nature*, **538**(7626), 510–513.

Slon, V., Mafessoni, F., Vernot, B. et al. (2018). The genome of the offspring of a Neanderthal mother and a Denisovan father. *Nature*, **561**(7721), 113–116.

Smith, J., Coop, G., Stephens, M., & Novembre, J. (2018). Estimating time to the common ancestor for a beneficial Allele. *Molecular Biology and Evolution*, **35**(4), 1003–1017.

Spengler, R., Frachetti, M., Doumani, P. et al. (2014a). Early agriculture and crop transmission among Bronze Age mobile pastoralists of Central Eurasia. *Proceedings of the Royal Society B: Biological Sciences*, **281**(1783), 20133382.

Spengler, R. N., Frachetti, M. D., & Doumani, P. N. (2014b). Late Bronze Age agriculture at Tasbas in the Dzhungar Mountains of eastern Kazakhstan. *Quaternary International*, **348**, 147–157.

Stoneking, M., & Delfin, F. (2010). The human genetic history of East Asia: Weaving a complex tapestry. *Current Biology*, **20**(4), R188–R193.

Sun, X., Wen, S., Lu, C. et al. (2021). Ancient DNA and multimethod dating confirm the late arrival of anatomically modern humans in southern China. *Proceedings of the National Academy of Sciences*, **118**(8), e2019158118.

Sun, Y., & Zhao, Z. (2013). 魏家窝铺红山文化遗址出土植物遗存综合研究 [Study of the plant remains unearthed at Weijiawopu, a Hongshan culture site]. *Nongye Kaogu (Agricultural Archaeology)*, **3**, 1–5.

Suzuki, H., & Hanihara, K. (Eds.). (1982). *The Minatogawa Man: The Upper Pleistocene Man from the Island of Okinawa*, Tokyo: University of Tokyo Press.

Taylor, W., Wilkin, S., Wright, J. et al. (2019). Radiocarbon dating and cultural dynamics across Mongolia's early pastoral transition. *PLoS ONE*, **14**(11), e0224241.

Teixeira, J. C., Jacobs, G. S., Stringer, C. et al. (2021). Widespread Denisovan ancestry in Island Southeast Asia but no evidence of substantial super-archaic hominin admixture. *Nature Ecology & Evolution*, **5**(5), 616–624.

Thornton, C. P., & Schurr, T. G. (2004). Genes, language, and culture: An example from the Tarim basin. *Oxford Journal of Archaeology*, **23**(1), 83–106.

Turner, C. G. (1987). Late Pleistocene and Holocene population history of east Asia based on dental variation. *American Journal of Physical Anthropology*, **73**(3), 305–321.

Vallini, L., Marciani, G., Aneli, S. et al. (2022). Genetics and material culture support repeated expansions into Paleolithic Eurasia from a population hub out of Africa. *Genome Biology and Evolution*, **14**(4), evac045.

van Driem, G. (2005). Tibeto-Burman vs. Indo-Chinese: Implications for population geneticists, archaeologists and prehistorians. In R. Blench & L. Sagart, eds., *The Peopling of East Asia: Putting Together Archaeology, Linguistics and Genetics*, London: RoutledgeCurzon, pp. 83–108.

Wall, J. D., & Kim, S. K. (2007). Inconsistencies in Neanderthal genomic DNA sequences. *PLoS Genetics*, **3**(10), e175.

Wang, C.-C., Yeh, H.-Y., Popov, A. N. et al. (2021a). Genomic insights into the formation of human populations in East Asia. *Nature*, **591**(7850), 413–419.

Wang, H., Yang, M. A., Wangdue, S. et al. (2023). Human genetic history on the Tibetan Plateau in the past 5100 years. *Science Advances*, **9**(11), eadd5582.

Wang, R., & Wang, C.-C. (2022). Human genetics: The dual origin of Three Kingdoms period Koreans. *Current Biology*, **32**(15), R844–R847.

Wang, T., Wang, W., Xie, G. et al. (2021b). Human population history at the crossroads of East and Southeast Asia since 11,000 years ago. *Cell*, **184**(14), 3829–3841.e21.

Wang, W., & Zhao, H. (2022). "中华文明探源工程" 及其主要收获 [Chinese civilization's origins project and its main achievements]. *Chinese History Research*, **4**, 5–32.

Watanabe, Y., Naka, I., Khor, S.-S. et al. (2019). Analysis of whole Y-chromosome sequences reveals the Japanese population history in the Jomon period. *Scientific Reports*, **9**(1), 8556.

Weisskopf, A., Deng, Z., Qin, L., & Fuller, D. Q. (2015). The interplay of millets and rice in Neolithic central China: Integrating phytoliths into the archaeobotany of Baligang. *Archaeological Research in Asia*, **4**, 36–45.

Welker, F., Ramos-Madrigal, J., Gutenbrunner, P. et al. (2020). The dental proteome of Homo antecessor. *Nature*, **580**(7802), 235–238.

Whitman, J. (2011). Northeast Asian linguistic ecology and the advent of rice agriculture in Korea and Japan. *Rice*, **4**(3–4), 149–158.

Wilkin, S., Ventresca Miller, A., Taylor, W. T. T. et al. (2020). Dairy pastoralism sustained eastern Eurasian steppe populations for 5,000 years. *Nature Ecology & Evolution*, **4**(3), 346–355.

Wright, J. (2021). Prehistoric Mongolian archaeology in the early 21st century: Developments in the steppe and beyond. *Journal of Archaeological Research*, **29**(3), 431–479.

Wright, J., Ganbaatar, G., Honeychurch, W., Byambatseren, B., & Rosen, A. (2019). The earliest Bronze Age culture of the south-eastern Gobi desert, Mongolia. *Antiquity*, **93**(368), 393–411.

Wu, C. (2021). A brief review on the researches of cultural relationship between Indigenous Bai Yue in Southeast of China and Pacific Austronesian. In C. Wu, ed., *The Prehistoric Maritime Frontier of Southeast China*, Vol. 4, Singapore: Springer Singapore, pp. 209–219.

Xiang, H., Gao, J., Yu, B. et al. (2014). Early Holocene chicken domestication in northern China. *Proceedings of the National Academy of Sciences*, **111** (49), 17564–17569.

Xiang, K., Ouzhuluobu, Peng, Y. et al. (2013). Identification of a Tibetan-Specific mutation in the Hypoxic gene EGLN1 and its contribution to high-altitude adaptation. *Molecular Biology and Evolution*, **30**(8), 1889–1898.

Xie, M., Yang, Y., Wang, B., & Wang, C. (2013). Interdisciplinary investigation on ancient *Ephedra* twigs from Gumugou Cemetery (3800b.p.) in Xinjiang region, northwest China: Identification on Ancient *Ephedra* in China. *Microscopy Research and Technique*, **76**(7), 663–672.

Yamaguchi, B. (1982). A Review of the osteological characteristics of the Jomon population in Prehistoric Japan. *Journal of the Anthropological Society of Nippon*, **90**(Supplement), 77–90.

Yan, Y., Ge, W., Wang, Y. et al. (2022). Determining the earliest directly dated cremation tombs in Neolithic China via multidisciplinary approaches: A case study at Laohudun site. *International Journal of Osteoarchaeology*, **32**(5), 1130–1141.

Yang, B., Shi, Y., Braeuning, A., & Wang, J. (2004). Evidence for a warm-humid climate in arid northwestern China during 40–30ka BP. *Quaternary Science Reviews*, **23**(23–24), 2537–2548.

Yang, L. (2014). Zhoukoudian: Geography and culture. In C. Smith, ed., *Encyclopedia of Global Archaeology*, New York: Springer New York, pp. 7961–7965.

Yang, M. A. (2022). A genetic history of migration, diversification, and admixture in Asia. *Human Population Genetics and Genomics*, **2**(1), 1–32.

Yang, M. A., Fan, X., Sun, B. et al. (2020). Ancient DNA indicates human population shifts and admixture in northern and southern China. *Science*, **369**(6501), 282–288.

Yang, M. A., Gao, X., Theunert, C. et al. (2017). 40,000-year-old individual from Asia provides insight into early population structure in Eurasia. *Current Biology*, **27**(20), 3202–3208.e9.

Yang, R., Yang, Y., Li, W. et al. (2014a). Investigation of cereal remains at the Xiaohe Cemetery in Xinjiang, China. *Journal of Archaeological Science*, **49**, 42–47.

Yang, Y., Shevchenko, A., Knaust, A. et al. (2014b). Proteomics evidence for kefir dairy in Early Bronze Age China. *Journal of Archaeological Science*, **45**, 178–186.

Zaim, Y., Ciochon, R. L., Polanski, J. M. et al. (2011). New 1.5 million-year-old Homo erectus maxilla from Sangiran (Central Java, Indonesia). *Journal of Human Evolution*, **61**(4), 363–376.

Zavala, E. I., Jacobs, Z., Vernot, B. et al. (2021). Pleistocene sediment DNA reveals hominin and faunal turnovers at Denisova Cave. *Nature*, **595**(7867), 399–403.

Zhang, D. D., Bennett, M. R., Cheng, H. et al. (2021a). Earliest parietal art: Hominin hand and foot traces from the middle Pleistocene of Tibet. *Science Bulletin*, **66**(24), 2506–2515.

Zhang, D., Xia, H., Chen, F. et al. (2020). Denisovan DNA in Late Pleistocene sediments from Baishiya Karst Cave on the Tibetan Plateau. *Science*, **370** (6516), 584–587.

Zhang, F., Ning, C., Scott, A. et al. (2021b). The genomic origins of the Bronze Age Tarim Basin mummies. *Nature*, **599**(7884), 256–261.

Zhang, M., Yan, S., Pan, W., & Jin, L. (2019). Phylogenetic evidence for Sino-Tibetan origin in northern China in the Late Neolithic. *Nature*, **569** (7754), 112–115.

Zhang, X. (2015). 大汶口文化研究 *[Dawenkou Culture Research] (Thesis)*, Jilin University.

Zhang, X. L., Ha, B. B., Wang, S. J. et al. (2018). The earliest human occupation of the high-altitude Tibetan Plateau 40 thousand to 30 thousand years ago. *Science*, **362**(6418), 1049–1051.

Zhang, X., Witt, K. E., Bañuelos, M. M., et al. (2021c). The History and evolution of the Denisovan- *EPAS1* haplotype in Tibetans. *Proceedings of the National Academy of Sciences*, **118**(22), e2020803118.

Zhang, Z. H. (1991). 中国考古学通论 *[Conspectus of Chinese Archaeology]*, Nanjing: Nanjing University Press.

Zhao, J., Hu, K., Collerson, K. D., & Xu, H. (2001). Thermal Ionization Mass Spectrometry U-Series Dating of a Hominid Site Near Nanjing, China. *Geology*, **29**(1), 27.

Zhao, M., Kong, Q.-P., Wang, H.-W. et al. (2009). Mitochondrial Genome Evidence Reveals Successful Late Paleolithic Settlement on the Tibetan Plateau. *Proceedings of the National Academy of Sciences*, **106**(50), 21230–21235.

Zhou, X., Yu, J., Spengler, R. N. et al. (2020). 5,200-Year-Old Cereal Grains from the Eastern Altai Mountains Redate the Trans-Eurasian Crop Exchange. *Nature Plants*, **6**, 78–87.

Zhu, J., Ma, J., Zhang, F. et al. (2021). The Baigetuobie Cemetery: New Discovery and Human Genetic Features of Andronovo Community's Diffusion to the Eastern Tianshan Mountains (1800–1500 BC). *The Holocene*, **31**(2), 217–229.

Zhu, Z., Dennell, R., Huang, W. et al. (2018). Hominin Occupation of the Chinese Loess Plateau since about 2.1 Million Years Ago. *Nature*, **559** (7715), 608–612.

Zhu, Z.-Y., Dennell, R., Huang, W.-W. et al. (2015). New Dating of the Homo Erectus Cranium from Lantian (Gongwangling), China. *Journal of Human Evolution*, **78**, 144–157.

Zwyns, N. (2021). The initial Upper Paleolithic in central and East Asia: Blade technology, cultural transmission, and implications for human dispersals. *Journal of Paleolithic Archaeology*, **4**(3), 19.

Zwyns, N., Gladyshev, S., Tabarev, A., & Gunchinsuren, B. (2014). Mongolia: Paleolithic. In C. Smith, ed., *Encyclopedia of Global Archaeology*, New York: Springer New York, pp. 5025–5032.

Zwyns, N., Paine, C. H., Tsedendorj, B. et al. (2019). The Northern route for human dispersal in Central and Northeast Asia: New evidence from the site of Tolbor-16, Mongolia. *Scientific Reports*, **9**(1), 11759.

Author Contributions

Conceptualization: E.A.B. and Q.F.; material contributions: Y.L.; writing, original draft: E.A.B. and Q.F.; reviewing and editing: E.A.B., and Q.F. E.A.B. and Q.F. contributed equally to the work.

Declaration of Interests

The authors declare no competing interests.

Acknowledgments

We acknowledge constructive discussions and feedback from the Molecular Paleontology Laboratory members at the IVPP. We especially thank Siqiong Liu, Shiyu Qiao, and Han Shi for their help in preparing materials. This work was supported by the National Natural Science Foundation of China (41925009), the Chinese Academy of Sciences (CAS) (YSBR019).

Cambridge Elements

Ancient East Asia

Erica Fox Brindley

Pennsylvania State University

Erica Fox Brindley is Professor and Head in the Department of Asian Studies at Pennsylvania State University. She is the author of three books, co-editor of several volumes, and the recipient of the ACLS Ryskamp Fellowship and Humboldt Fellowship. Her research focuses on the history of the self, knowledge, music, and identity in ancient China, as well as on the history of the Yue/Viet cultures from southern China and Vietnam.

Rowan Kimon Flad

Harvard University

Rowan Kimon Flad is the John E. Hudson Professor of Archaeology in the Department of Anthropology at Harvard University. He has authored two books and over 50 articles, edited several volumes, and served as editor of Asian Perspectives. His archaeological research focuses on economic and ritual activity, interregional interaction, and technological and environmental change, in the late Neolithic and early Bronze Ages of the Sichuan Basin and the Upper Yellow River valley regions of China.

About the Series

Elements in Ancient East Asia contains multi-disciplinary contributions focusing on the history and culture of East Asia in ancient times. Its framework extends beyond anachronistic, nation-based conceptions of the past, following instead the contours of Asian sub-regions and their interconnections with each other. Within the series there are five thematic groups: 'Sources', which includes excavated texts and other new sources of data; 'Environments', exploring interaction zones of ancient East Asia and long-distance connections; 'Institutions', including the state and its military; 'People', including family, gender, class, and the individual and 'Ideas', concerning religion and philosophy, as well as the arts and sciences. The series presents the latest findings and strikingly new perspectives on the ancient world in East Asia.

Cambridge Elements

Ancient East Asia

Elements in the Series

A full series listing is available at: www.cambridge.org/EAEA

Printed in the United States
by Baker & Taylor Publisher Services